MEDITERRANEAN

REFRESH COOKBOOK

FOR BEGINNERS 2024

**The Mediterranean Diet Made Easy, Quick and Tasty:
Delicious Recipes for Optimal Health**

WILLIAM C. GOBER

CONTENTS

INTRODUCTION

Gather 'round, friends, because I bring news of sun-drenched coasts and olive-oil-kissed joys! This isn't your average cookbook, believe me. No, this is an odyssey, a culinary journey to realms where ancient gods' whispers blend with the laughter of fishermen mending their nets. It's a flavor symphony, an explosion of fresh citrus and fragrant herbs on a stage drenched in the golden light of the Mediterranean sun.

Some may argue that the Mediterranean diet is simply a fancy way of stating "eat vegetables and olive oil." But what a universe one simple statement opens up! It's like a kaleidoscope, with brilliant scarlet tomatoes nestled alongside pearly white feta, plump Kalamata olives winking from salty salads, and fluffy pita bread demanding to be dunked in garlicky hummus at every turn. Every bite is a discovery, a tribute to the simple reality that using fresh, seasonal ingredients and preparing them with love and a dash of whimsy can turn a dinner into a celebration.

But hold on, there's more! This is more than simply a cookbook; it's a gateway to a way of life. It's about long lunches under grapevines, laughing reverberating between sun-baked dwellings, and the clinking of glasses raised to toast excellent food, good company, and the sheer joy of being alive. It's about sharing plates with loved ones, telling stories with each bite, and knowing that a meal is always more than the sum of its parts.

So, dear friends, open this book and allow it to transport you. Allow the aromas of rosemary and thyme to fill your home, the tang of lemon to dance on your tongue, and the warmth of the Mediterranean sun to fill your soul. For within these pages is a promise, a promise of vivid life, shared laughter, and the wonderful, refreshing vacation that only a Mediterranean feast can provide.

Now that we've finished talking, let's eat! Turn the page, grab your apron, and prepare to be astonished by the culinary symphony that awaits.

SEIZE THE PLENTY:

- **Freshness is king:** Imagine light salads brimming with in-season produce like sun-dappled tomatoes, luscious melons, and crispy cucumbers. Picture light and airy pita bread, fresh out of the oven, dipped in smooth and creamy hummus produced from chickpeas cultivated in the Mediterranean climate.
- **A celebration driven by plants**: nutritious grains, legumes, and vegetables take center stage. Imagine robust stews of lentils cooked with herbs, light pilafs of quinoa flecked with spices and almonds, and spaghetti mixed with grilled eggplant and zucchini.
- **Good fats for the win:** Your cooking partner should be extra virgin olive oil, the liquid gold of the Mediterranean. For a burst of antioxidants and a taste of sunshine, drizzle it over salads, toast, and veggies.

MINDFUL INDULGENCE:

- **Dairy and meat are only passing visitors, not the main attraction:** Dairy and meat are not eliminated, but they are relegated. Imagine a dab of tart Greek yogurt served with fresh fruit, or lean fish grilled with lemon and herbs. By taking a deliberate approach, you may enjoy these complex tastes without going overboard.
- **Guilt-free sweet satisfaction:** The sweetness of ripe fruit brings life to desserts. Consider luscious fruit compotes, berry-topped yogurt parfaits, or airy baklava with honey sprinkled over flaky phyllo pastry.
- **Leading the Life:** • Going Above and Beyond: There's more to the Mediterranean Refresh than meets the eye. It's about appreciating life's little joys, relishing meals with loved ones, and accepting a slower pace of existence. Imagine strolling down the shore at a leisurely pace, enjoying herbal tea under the olive trees, or cracking jokes over mezze platters.

The Mediterranean Refresh Diet is ultimately a call to rediscover the pleasures of a nutritious diet. It's about enjoying the natural beauty and cultural diversity of the Mediterranean lifestyle while providing your body with wholesome, delectable cuisine. Now shut your eyes, take a deep breath, and picture yourself walking into that sun-filled kitchen. The Mediterranean Refresh Diet is here to take you on a delectable trip to a better, happier version of yourself.

- **HAPPIER DANCING, STRONGER HEART**: This diet takes good care of your heart, much as a devoted gardener would. You can dance to the beat of a healthy life as studies reveal it decreases bad cholesterol, regulates blood pressure, and lowers the risk of heart disease.

- **BLOOMS OF BRAINPOWER**: Think of your brain as a vibrant neuronal garden that is flourishing in the Mediterranean climate. This diet may prevent Alzheimer's and cognitive decline, keeping your mind active and interesting for years to come, according to research.

- **TANGO IN YOUR STOMACH:** Visualize your stomach as a busy marketplace where beneficial bacteria host a happy celebration. These little companions are nourished by the fiber-rich richness of the Mediterranean Diet, which results in improved digestion, a flatter stomach, and less bloating.

- **THE WEIGHT-LOSS WALTZ:** Lose extra pounds by dancing away your tension. With none of the drama associated with fad diets, this diet places an emphasis on complete, unprocessed meals that keep you feeling full and aid in natural weight management.

- **MOVE TO THE MUSIC:** Experience the energy of the Mediterranean sun with each stride. This diet provides your body with the necessary vitamins, complex carbs, and healthy fats it needs to function, leaving you feeling energised and prepared to take on the day.

- **MOOD SWINGS TAKE A NAP:** Visualize tension dissipating like heat under a refreshing evening breeze. A calmer, more balanced mood may result from the Mediterranean Diet, which is high in antioxidants and omega-3 fatty acids and supports brain health and wellbeing.

- **SLEEP TURNS INTO A CALM SYMPHONY:** Imagine drifting off to slumber as the soft sound of the Mediterranean waves lulls you to sleep. By encouraging the generation of melatonin, this diet supports appropriate sleep patterns, ensuring that you wake up feeling refreshed and invigorated.

- **GASTRONOMIC EXPLORATION**: Picture your palate on a Mediterranean vacation and enjoying a rainbow of tastes. From the zesty taste of lemon on grilled fish to the comforting creamy hummus and the sweetness of sun-ripened fruit, every meal turns into an adventure.

- **SHARING TURNS BECOMES A FEAST**: Imagine happy laughing reverberating over a table covered with vibrant food. This diet is about uniting people to celebrate life and share the abundance of the planet over delectable food, not only about personal health.

- **ENDURING HAPPINESS**: Do away with fad diets that make you feel unhappy and cheated. The Mediterranean Refresh Diet is not a quick remedy; rather, it is a way of life. It's an encouragement to adopt easy, long-lasting healthy behaviors that will contribute to your lifelong wellbeing.

FRESHNESS IS EVERYTHING:

- **VEGETABLES**: Imagine colorful plates piled high with in-season gems such as snappy carrots, juicy tomatoes, sweet peppers, and crisp cucumbers. Imagine colorful salads that may be made from lush greens like spinach and kale. Remember those aromatic herbs that may give any food a taste boost, such as thyme, basil, and oregano.

- **FRUITS**: Suck in the sweetness of sun-ripened peaches, juicy berries, and zesty citrus fruits—nature's candies. Accept the acidic joy of pomegranates or the sweetness of watermelon. These beauties infuse every meal with vitamins, fiber, and a hint of sunlight.

- **LEGUMES & WHOLE GRAINS:** When simmered in substantial stews or blended into creamy dips, lentils, chickpeas, and beans provide protein and fiber to your diet. Complex carbs included in whole-wheat bread, quinoa, and brown rice provide long-lasting energy and are ideal for constructing filling meals.

- **NUTS & SEEDS**: Pine nuts, almonds, walnuts, and pistachios provide salads, dips, and even desserts a unique tactile element and healthful fats. Sprinkle in nutrient and flavorful bursts from sunflower and sesame seeds.

GOOD FATS TO THE RESCUE:

• **OLIVE OIL**: Your culinary best buddy is this liquid treasure from the Mediterranean. Pour it over veggies, toast, and salads to provide a hint of sunshine and heart-healthy monounsaturated fats.

Appreciating the Extras

• **GARLIC AND ONIONS**: These flavorful main ingredients give stews, sauces, and roasted veggies their depth and coziness. They are the foundation of many Mediterranean meals.

• HERBS & SPICES: The key to discovering new and exotic tastes is a well-stocked spice cupboard. Try blending different spices such as paprika, cumin, cinnamon, and turmeric to discover the unique flavors of the area. Herbs that are in season such as parsley, mint, and dill give your meals a vivid, fresh taste.

• CHEESE AND YOGURT: Savor these dairy products in moderation. Greek yogurt works well as a creamy foundation for sauces, dips, and even desserts. Cheeses like feta, ricotta, and halloumi give salads, pastas, and grilled foods a hint of richness and a salty taste.

YOUR KITCHEN COMPANIONS: YOUR TRADE TOOLS

• POINTY BLADES: Easy dicing, slicing, and chopping requires a fine chef's knife and paring knife. To ensure safety and convenience of usage, buy high-quality blades and maintain them sharp.

• BOARDS FOR CUTTING: To keep your counters clean and safe, choose cutting boards made of strong plastic or wood. In order to avoid cross-contamination, think about using different boards for meat and veggies.

• **LARGE POT & SKILLET**: Pan-frying, stir-frying, soups, and stews all need a flexible pot and skillet. Select oven-safe choices to increase your cooking versatility.

• SALAD SPINNER & SERVING PLATTERS: Stylish serving platters enhance your meals and wow your visitors, while a salad spinner keeps greens fresh and dry.

• CITRUS JUICER & MICROPLANE: Invigorating marinades, sauces, and drinks are enhanced with freshly squeezed lemon and orange juice. An additional layer of flavor is added by using a microplane zester to liberate the fragrant oils from citrus rinds.

• **MEASURING SPOONS AND OLIVE OIL DISPENSERS**: Measuring spoons guarantee precise measurements for recipes, while olive oil dispensers assist you in drizzling the ideal quantity.

Past the Pantry:

• **STUNNING SERVING PIECES**: Adopt the Mediterranean custom of dining with close companions. Invest in vibrant bowls, plates, and silverware to elevate every meal into a festive occasion.

• **COOKBOOKS & ONLINE RESOURCES**: There are a tonne of resources out there to help you along the way when it comes to cooking. For ideas, peruse cookbooks, investigate internet recipe repositories, and adhere to Mediterranean food bloggers.

• PLAYFUL SPIRIT & OPEN MIND: Don't be scared to try new things! This is not a science experiment; rather, it is a culinary excursion. Play around with tastes, experiment with new ingredients, and enjoy yourself in the kitchen.

COMPREHENDING THE MEDITERRANEAN WAY OF LIFE

The Mediterranean lifestyle is a symphony of sun-kissed behaviors that come together to produce a happier, healthier way of life. It's not just about eating. Picture yourself being taken to a whitewashed town with a view of the sparkling Aegean Sea, where the scent of sea salt and fresh herbs fills the air. Here's a closer look at the crucial components that compose this catchy melody:

FOOD FOR BOTH THE BODY AND THE SOUL:

• **PRIORITIZING FRESHNESS**: Imagine bright salads full of fresh veggies, sun-ripened fruit that is glistening with sugar, and nutritious grains cooked in aromatic stews. This diet emphasizes the use of fresh, unprocessed foods, allowing the abundance of nature to take center stage.

• OLIVE OIL, THE PRECIOUS MINERAL: Drizzle bread, veggies, and salads with this sun-like healthful fat. It is more than simply a utensil in the kitchen; it is a representation of the Mediterranean lifestyle and gives every meal a richer taste.

• MINDFUL MODERATION: Meat and dairy take a backseat, showing up in lower serving sizes and often combined with starchy plants. Eating with mindfulness promotes a balanced and fulfilling diet by prioritizing quality over quantity.

• SLOW CUISINE, QUICK JOY: Spend some time enjoying your food. Savor calm mornings drenched in morning sunlight, family feasts full of laughter, and leisurely lunches with friends. Meals start to become more than simply a source of energy.

MOVING PAST THE PLATE: ACCEPTING THE JOY OF LIFE

• MOTION FEATURING A MEDITERRANEAN FLAIR: Put an end to your rigorous workouts. Imagine bike rides through olive orchards, languid stroll along the shore, and spontaneous dance parties that are powered by music and joy. Moving becomes a joy of life rather than a burden.

• SOAKING UP THE SUN: The Mediterranean sun is a natural mood enhancer in addition to being a source of warmth. Enjoy a walk in the evening or a cup of coffee in the morning, and let the sun revitalize your body and soul.

• FAMILY IS THE COMMUNITY: A fundamental aspect of the Mediterranean lifestyle is dining together with loved ones. Imagine animated discussions during swims and bursts of laughter from balconies covered with vines that bloom. Just as food nurtures the body, community nourishes the spirit.

• SIESTA, SWEET SIESTA: Savor the afternoon break as a chance to unwind, rejuvenate, and reestablish personal connections. This noon break is a celebration of slowing down and enjoying life's little joys, not a time to be lazy.

LIVING PURPOSEFULLY:

• SUSTAINABILITY & SIMPLICITY: Reduce waste, support your community, and recognize the worth of handcrafted, basic items. With its emphasis on mindful consumerism and leisurely living, this way of life leaves less of an environmental impact.

• EXISTING IN THE NOW: Turn off the incessant hum of technology and concentrate on the present moment. Savor the flavor of your meal, the sun's warmth, and the company of those you love laughing. Let the enchantment of the Mediterranean work its spell as you stay in the present.

THE ESSENTIALS OF MEDITERRANEAN COOKING

REVEALING THE MEDITERRANEAN FEAST: An Exploration of the Fundamentals of Cooking

Rather from being a single dish, Mediterranean food is a lively tapestry that reflects the traditions and tastes of sun-drenched nations that border the azure waters of the sea that gives its name. Every country contributes a different element to the culinary tapestry, resulting in a symphony of flavors that satisfies the mind and body. Examples of these regions include the rolling vineyards of Italy, the bustling souks of Morocco, the olive orchards of Greece, and the spice-filled marketplaces of Turkey. Examining the fundamentals of this cuisine will take you on a delectable voyage as you discover the essential components, techniques, and customs that characterize this eating style.

THE TRINITY OF FLAVOR: The olive, the wheat, and the wine are the three fundamental components that welcome you as soon as you enter the sun-drenched Mediterranean kitchen. These "trinity" elements, which may be found in a myriad of forms and combinations, serve as the cornerstone of the cuisine.

• THE OLIVE: Its abundance produces olive oil, the liquid gold of the Mediterranean. Drizzled over bread, veggies, and salads, it gives food a velvety, rich taste and adds to the area's well-known heart-healthy diet. The actual olives, whether brine-cured or preserved with herbs and spices, provide a saline, salty contrast to a variety of foods.

• THE WHEAT: Wheat flour may be found in a wide variety of dishes, such as crisp flatbreads like lavash and airy pita bread, as well as rustic loaves full of delicious crust. Pasta swirls in bright sauces in an infinite variety of shapes and sizes, while couscous adds a light, fluffy texture to stews and salads.

• THE GRAPE: Not only is wine a beverage, but it also finds its way into food preparations from the sun-kissed vineyards. White wine lends acidity to sauces, red wine simmers well with braising liquids, and raisins are used in both savory and sweet recipes.

A FRESH COLOR SCHEME: The Mediterranean table's core rotates in time with the seasons. A rainbow of colors created by sun-drenched and perfectly harvested veggies may be found in a plethora of meals. Roasted tomatoes blend well with sweet peppers and aromatic garlic, leafy greens become refreshing salads, and eggplant is a treat in a variety of stews, dips, and even as the centerpiece of the traditional Greek meal moussaka.

A SYMPHONY OF SEASONINGS: When it comes to herbs and spices, Mediterranean cookery isn't afraid to use them. Herbs such as oregano, thyme, rosemary, and basil fill the air, each adding a distinct scent to food preparation. Salads benefit from the zest of mint, grilled meats get a smokey warmth from paprika, and Moroccan tagines dance with the dance of cumin and coriander. Paella benefits from the delicate golden color and delicate flowery scent of saffron, while sweet delights are warmed by the warmth of cloves and cinnamon.

BEYOND THE PLATE: CUSTOMS AND HOLIDAYS

In the Mediterranean, food is more than just a source of nourishment; it is a social construct that is revered by long-standing customs. Around mezze tables, which are filled with a variety of tiny morsels designed to be shared and enjoyed, families congregate. Meals are now relaxed events that are accompanied by discussion and laughter. They may be taken outside in the warm sun or by candlelight.

There are special culinary manifestations for religious occasions. Greek Easter tables are adorned with sweet baklava, while Moroccan Eid al-Fitr is celebrated with aromatic stews of lamb. Meals also provides a rhythm to daily routines. Honey-drizzled yogurt or fresh fruit are served with afternoon siestas, while thick and foamy coffee powers morning conversation.

EMBRACING THE MEDITERRANEAN SPIRIT: Mediterranean cuisine is more than simply a compilation of ingredients and cooking techniques; it is a way of life. It's about appreciating the act of dining with loved ones, relishing uncomplicated, fresh tastes, and respecting the cycles of everyday life and the natural world. It's about enjoying the pleasure of sharing a meal with others, cooking with purpose, and utilizing high-quality products.

Now enter the Mediterranean kitchen, bathed in sunshine. Allow the perfume of spices and herbs to lead the way, be drawn in by the vivid hues of fresh food, and feel the warmth of the community as you arrive. One delectable mouthful at a time, discover the culinary mysteries of this long-standing and diversified heritage. Recall that the real beauty of food is not just in its ability to unite people, feed the spirit, and celebrate life's little joys.

ESSENTIAL ELEMENTS OF A MEDITERRANEAN DIET

A FESTIVITY OF PLANT-BASED ENERGY:

• **Fruits & Veggies**: Imagine a rainbow consisting of flavorful herbs mingling with crunchy cucumbers, juicy tomatoes, sweet peppers, and verdant greens on your dish. Fruits provide a symphony of sweetness and nutrition, from citrus bursts to sun-ripened peaches. These stars of the plant world take center stage, providing your body with vitamins, fiber, and eye-catching hues.

• **Legumes & Whole Grains**: Beans, lentils, and chickpeas join the party as warriors of protein and fiber that can be combined into creamy dips or simmered in substantial stews. Complex carbs found in whole-wheat bread, quinoa, and brown rice provide long-lasting energy and provide the groundwork for wholesome, filling meals.

ENERGETIC FATS, TASTY DIPS:

• **Olive oil**: More than simply a condiment, this liquid gold of the Mediterranean is a culinary partner. Pour it over veggies, toast, and salads to provide a hint of sunshine and heart-healthy monounsaturated fats. Because of its excellent taste and health advantages, go for extra virgin olive oil.

APPRECIATING THE EXTRAS

• **Fish & Seafood**: Imagine delicately boiled mussels dipped in white wine, or grilled sardines gleaming with lemon. When consumed in moderation, fish and seafood provide protein, healthy omega-3 fatty acids, and a hint of the ocean.

• **Dairy & Eggs**: Eggs provide protein and variety, while yogurt and cheese give meals a delicious creaminess. Savor these treats in moderation to appreciate their richness without going overboard.

PAST THE PLATE: HEALTHY ROUTINES FOR THE BODY AND MIND:

• **Mindful Moderation**: Strict guidelines or starvation are not part of the Mediterranean Diet. It's about eating with awareness, indulging in delights from time to time, and paying attention to general dietary habits.

• **Seasonal Feasts**: Savor the finest foods at the peak of freshness. Enjoy the rich tomatoes of summer and the robust greens of winter, allowing the seasons to influence your cooking choices.

• **Community & Connection**: Sharing food with loved ones turns it into a celebration. Savor the thrill of cooking and dining together, as well as relaxed dinners and lively get-togethers.

• **Activity & Movement**: Living a Mediterranean lifestyle involves more than simply eating. Take leisurely strolls in the sunlight, go on bike rides, or even just dance in the kitchen.

THE SECRET IS IN THE DETAILS

AN EXPLORATION INTO MEDITERRANEAN CUISINE

Come on a voyage with me, my dear buddy, where the air is filled with the aroma of thyme and rosemary and sun-kissed olives shimmer against azure waters. We're enjoying the flavors that have been teasing palates for generations as we travel through colorful landscapes and historic towns on a gourmet tour of the Mediterranean.

Imagine meandering through thriving Moroccan marketplaces, where the perfume of potent spices such as saffron and cumin fills the air. We will have warm mint tea while snacking on sticky baklava, which has layers coated in honey and topped with crunchy almonds. With a symphony of flavors in every mouthful, we will indulge in aromatic tagines loaded with delicate lamb and sweet prunes as the sun sets, creating long shadows over the terracotta roofs.

Then, when we get closer to Greece's sun-kissed coastline, we'll sail across the Aegean, the salty wind tearing through our hair. We will feast on dishes full of tender grilled octopus drenched in olive oil and lemon juice, accompanied by tart feta cheese and crunchy cucumber slices, in charming tavernas with walls painted blue and white. We'll raise glasses of ouzo, the sea's perfume evoked by its aniseed notes, and relish the flavor of history with each sip.

The scent of wood-fired ovens entices us to trattorias hidden along cobblestone lanes in Italy. We'll eat platters of al dente pasta covered in rich, slow-cooked tomato sauces or sprinkled in colorful pesto. Imagine our tongues tasting the combination of earthy and sunny flavors as we bite into chewy focaccia coated in aromatic olive oil. Every mouthful bears witness to the Italian passion for using seasonal, fresh ingredients.

As one travels around Spain, the sound of flamenco dancers fills tapas establishments to the brim with vibrant treats. We'll pass around platters of crunchy patatas bravas dipped in spicy aioli, poppable plump piquillo peppers packed with creamy goat cheese, and taste salty Manchego cheese. We'll hoist glasses of sangria as the night grows longer; the lively environment perfectly complements the sweet and fruity concoction.

We go on down the French Riviera, where the sea air is mixed with the aroma of lavender. We'll luxuriate in flaky croissants dunked in thick café au lait in sun-filled cafés, the buttery pastry melting on our lips like a sinful treat. Later, sophisticated dining establishments will entice us with subtle Provençal tastes, such as fresh ratatouille loaded with summer vegetables and fragrant lamb chops covered with herbs.

This, my friend, is just a small sampling of the Mediterranean's rich gastronomic tapestry. Every mouthful serves as a window into a distinct culture and a fork-tip tale passed down through the ages. We set out on a fresh journey with each meal, uncovering the essence of a millennium of sun-drenched years in every mouthwatering bite.

Are you prepared to go off on this gastronomic journey now? Prepare your palate for a voyage through flavorful landscapes where the sea whispers in every grain of salt, the sun caresses every olive, and the perfume of herbs leads us to tables heaped with the bounty of the Mediterranean. Cheers to your appetite!

CHAPTER ONE

BREAKFAST

1. SUN-KISSED TOMATO BRUSCHETTA WITH RICOTTA & HERBS

2. SPICED CHICKPEA SCRAMBLE WITH SPINACH & FETA

3. GREEK YOGURT PARFAIT WITH BERRIES & HONEY

4. BAKED EGGS WITH OLIVES & PEPPERS

5. MEDITERRANEAN TUNA SALAD ON WHOLE WHEAT TOAST

6. SMOOTHIE BOWL WITH SPINACH, BANANA, & MEDJOOL DATES

7. HONEYED BAKED APPLES WITH NUTS & YOGURT

8. MEDITERRANEAN OMELETTE WITH ZUCCHINI & GOAT CHEESE

9. OVERNIGHT OATS WITH FIGS & PISTACHIOS

10. BREAKFAST BRUSCHETTA WITH AVOCADO & SMOKED SALMON

SUN- KISSED TOMATO BRUSCHETTA WITH RICOTTA & HERBS

Prep Time: 10 minutes, **Cooking Time**: 15 minutes, **Total Time**: 25 minutes, **Servings**: 4-6

Ingredients:

- 1 baguette, sliced into 1/2-inch thick pieces
- 2 tablespoons olive oil
- 2 cloves garlic, minced
- 2 large ripe tomatoes, seeded and diced
- 1/2 cup ricotta cheese
- 1/4 cup chopped fresh basil

- 1 tablespoon chopped fresh oregano
- 1/4 teaspoon salt
- Pinch of black pepper
- Extra virgin olive oil, for drizzling
- Balsamic glaze, optional

Method:

1. Preheat oven to 400°F (200°C). Brush both sides of the bread slices with olive oil. Arrange on a baking sheet and toast in the oven for 10-15 minutes, flipping halfway through, until golden brown and crispy.

2. While the bread is toasting, heat the remaining olive oil in a skillet over medium heat. Add the garlic and cook for 30 seconds, until fragrant. Stir in the diced tomatoes and cook for 5-7 minutes, until softened and slightly juicy. Season with salt and pepper.

3. In a separate bowl, combine the ricotta cheese, basil, oregano, salt, and pepper. Stir gently until well combined.

4. To assemble, top each toasted bread slice with a spoonful of ricotta mixture. Spoon the warm tomato mixture on top of the ricotta. Drizzle with extra virgin olive oil and a touch of balsamic glaze, if desired. Serve immediately.

NUTRITIONAL INFORMATION : Calories: 250, Fat: 10g, Saturated Fat: 2g, Cholesterol: 15mg, Sodium: 250mg, Carbohydrates: 30g, Fiber: 2g, Sugar: 5g, Protein: 6g

SPICED CHICKPEA SCRAMBLE WITH SPINACH & FETA

Prep Time: 10 minutes, **Cooking Time**: 15 minutes, **Total Time:** 25 minutes, **Servings**: 2-3

Ingredients:

- 1 can of chickpeas, drained and rinsed
- 1 tablespoon olive oil
- 1/2 onion, chopped
- 2 cloves garlic, minced
- 1/2 teaspoon ground cumin
- 1/4 teaspoon turmeric
- Pinch of paprika
- 1/4 cup vegetable broth
- 1/2 cup chopped spinach
- 1/4 cup crumbled feta cheese
- Salt and black pepper to taste
- Cilantro leaves, chopped (optional)

Method:

1. In a large bowl, mash the chickpeas with a fork or potato masher until coarsely mashed, leaving some larger chunks for texture.
2. Heat olive oil in a skillet over medium heat. Add the onion and cook for 5-7 minutes, until softened and translucent. Add the garlic and cook for another minute, until fragrant.
3. Stir in the cumin, turmeric, and paprika, cook for 30 seconds to release the spices' aroma.
4. Add the mashed chickpeas and vegetable broth to the skillet. Stir to combine and cook for 5-7 minutes, until heated through and lightly browned.
5. Stir in the spinach and cook for another minute, until wilted.
6. Remove from heat and crumble the feta cheese on top. Season with salt and pepper to taste.
7. Serve immediately on toast, pita bread, or with a side of roasted vegetables. Garnish with chopped cilantro, if desired.

NUTRITIONAL INFORMATION : Calories: 300, Fat: 10g, Saturated Fat: 1g, Cholesterol: 0mg, Sodium: 300mg, Carbohydrates: 35g, Fiber: 10g, Sugar: 5g, Protein: 15g

GREEK YOGURT PARFAIT WITH BERRIES & HONEY   AND BAKED EGGS WITH OLIVES & PEPPERS

Prep Time: 5 minutes, **Cooking Time**: 0 minutes, **Total Time**: 5 minutes, **Servings**: 2

Ingredients:

- 1 cup plain Greek yogurt
- 1/2 cup fresh berries (blueberries, raspberries, strawberries, etc.)
- 1 tablespoon honey
- 1/4 cup granola (optional)
- Mint leaves, for garnish (optional)

Method:

1. Divide the yogurt evenly between two glasses or bowls.
2. Top each with half of the berries.
3. Drizzle each with honey.
4. Sprinkle with granola, if desired.
5. Garnish with mint leaves, if using.
6. Honey-Baked Eggs with Olives & Peppers

Prep Time: 5 minutes, **Cooking Time**: 15 minutes, **Total Time**: 20 minutes, **Servings**: 2

Ingredients:

- 2 eggs
- 2 tablespoons olive oil
- 1/2 red bell pepper, chopped
- 1/4 cup Kalamata olives, pitted and halved
- 1/4 teaspoon dried oregano
- Salt and black pepper to taste
- Fresh parsley, chopped (optional)

- Method:
- Preheat oven to 400°F (200°C).
- Divide the olive oil between two small oven-safe dishes or ramekins.
- Add the bell pepper and olives to each dish.
- Crack an egg into each dish, ensuring the yolk remains intact.

- Sprinkle with oregano, salt, and pepper.

- Bake for 12-15 minutes, until the whites are set and the yolks are slightly runny.

- Garnish with chopped parsley, if desired.

NUTRITIONAL INFORMATION : Greek Yogurt Parfait: Calories: 250, Fat: 8g, Saturated Fat: 3g, Cholesterol: 20mg, Sodium: 150mg, Carbohydrates: 30g, Fiber: 2g,Sugar: 10g, Protein: 15g

Honey-Baked Eggs with Olives & Peppers: Calories: 280, Fat: 20g, Saturated Fat: 3g, Cholesterol: 185mg, Sodium: 300mg, Carbohydrates: 5g, Fiber: 1g Sugar: 2g, Protein: 12g

MEDITERRANEAN TUNA SALAD ON WHOLE WHEAT TOAST

Prep Time: 10 minutes **Cooking Time:** 0 minutes (optional) **Total Time:** 10 minutes Servings: 2

Ingredients:

- 2 cans (5 oz each) tuna packed in water, drained and flaked
- 1/4 cup chopped cherry tomatoes
- 1/4 cup chopped cucumber
- 1/4 cup chopped red onion
- 1/4 cup chopped Kalamata olives
- 1 tablespoon olive oil
- 1 tablespoon lemon juice
- 1 tablespoon chopped fresh parsley
- 1/2 teaspoon dried oregano
- Salt and black pepper to taste
- 2 slices whole wheat toast

Method:

1. In a medium bowl, combine the flaked tuna, cherry tomatoes, cucumber, red onion, and Kalamata olives.
2. In a separate bowl, whisk together the olive oil, lemon juice, parsley, oregano, salt, and pepper.
3. Pour the dressing over the tuna mixture and toss gently to combine.
4. Toast the whole wheat bread slices to your desired doneness.
5. Divide the tuna salad evenly between the toast slices.
6. Serve immediately and enjoy!

NUTRITIONAL INFORMATION : Calories: 400, Fat: 15g, Saturated Fat: 2g, Cholesterol: 80mg, Sodium: 400mg, Carbohydrates: 40g, Fiber: 5g, Sugar: 5g, Protein: 30g

SMOOTHIE BOWL WITH SPINACH, BANANA, & MEDJOOL DATES

Prep Time: 5 minutes **Blending Time**: 2 minutes **Total Time**: 7 minutes **Servings**: 1

Ingredients:

- 1 cup packed fresh spinach
- 1 frozen banana
- 2 Medjool dates, pitted and chopped
- 1 cup plant-based milk (almond, soy, coconut, etc.)
- 1/2 teaspoon vanilla extract (optional)
- 1/4 cup sliced fresh berries or chopped fruits (optional)
- Granola or shredded coconut, for topping (optional)
- Chopped nuts or seeds, for topping (optional)

Method:

1. Add the spinach, banana, dates, and plant-based milk to a blender.
2. Include vanilla extract if using.
3. Blend on high speed until smooth and creamy, around 2 minutes.
4. Pour the smoothie into a bowl.
5. Top with chopped berries or fruits, granola or shredded coconut, and nuts or seeds of your choice, if desired.
6. Enjoy your vibrant and delicious smoothie bowl!

NUTRITIONAL INFORMATION (APPROXIMATE) : Calories: 350, Fat: 10g, Saturated Fat: 2g,

Cholesterol: 0mg, Sodium: 150mg, Carbohydrates: 55g, Fiber: 8g, Sugar: 35g, Protein: 8g

Prep Time: 15 minutes **Cooking Time:** 40-45 minutes **Total Time**: 55-60 minutes **Servings**: 4

Ingredients:

- 4 apples (Granny Smith, Honeycrisp, or similar baking apples)
- 2 tablespoons lemon juice
- 1/4 cup honey
- 1/4 cup chopped walnuts or pecans
- 1/4 teaspoon ground cinnamon
- Pinch of salt
- 1 tablespoon butter, melted (optional)
- 1 cup plain Greek yogurt
- Drizzle of honey, for garnish (optional)

Method:

1. Preheat oven to 375°F (190°C).
2. Core the apples, leaving the bottoms intact. Drizzle with lemon juice to prevent browning.
3. In a small bowl, mix together the honey, nuts, cinnamon, and salt.
4. Fill each apple core with the nut mixture. Drizzle with melted butter, if using.
5. Place the apples in a baking dish and bake for 40-45 minutes, until tender and slightly golden.
6. While the apples bake, prepare the yogurt by stirring in a drizzle of honey, if desired.
7. Once baked, let the apples cool slightly before serving.
8. Spoon the Greek yogurt onto plates and top with a baked apple. Drizzle with additional honey, if desired.

NUTRITIONAL INFORMATION (PER SERVING, APPROXIMATE) : Calories: 300, Fat: 10g, Saturated Fat: 2g, Cholesterol: 15mg, Sodium: 150mg, Carbohydrates: 45g, Fiber: 5g, Sugar: 25g, Protein: 10g

MEDITERRANEAN OMELETTE WITH ZUCCHINI & GOAT CHEESE

Prep Time: 10 minutes **Cooking Time**: 12-15 minutes **Total Time**: 22-25 minutes **Servings**: 1

Ingredients:

- 2 eggs
- 1 tablespoon olive oil
- 1/2 small zucchini, thinly sliced
- 1/4 cup crumbled goat cheese
- 1 tablespoon chopped fresh parsley
- Salt and black pepper to taste
- Optional toppings: fresh basil, cherry tomatoes, sliced olives

Method:

1. In a small bowl, whisk together the eggs with a splash of water. Season with salt and pepper.
2. Heat olive oil in a non-stick frying pan over medium heat. Add the zucchini slices and cook for 2-3 minutes, until softened slightly.
3. Pour in the egg mixture, swirling the pan to evenly distribute. Let cook for about 1 minute, until the edges begin to set.
4. Sprinkle the goat cheese and parsley over one half of the omelette.
5. Using a spatula, fold the other half over the filling to create a crescent shape.
6. Cook for another minute or two, until the omelette is cooked through and slightly golden brown.
7. Slide the omelette onto a plate and garnish with your chosen toppings, if desired.

NUTRITIONAL INFORMATION (APPROXIMATE) : Calories: 300, Fat: 15g, Saturated Fat: 3g, Cholesterol: 200mg, Sodium: 300mg, Carbohydrates: 10g, Fiber: 2g, Sugar: 5g, Protein: 20g

OVERNIGHT OATS WITH FIGS & PISTACHIOS

Prep Time: 10 minutes **Cooking Time**: 0 minutes (overnight refrigeration) **Total Time:** 10 minutes (prep) + 8 hours (refrigeration) **Servings**: 1 generous portion

Ingredients:

- 1/2 cup rolled oats
- 1/3 cup milk (dairy or plant-based)
- 1/4 cup Greek yogurt (plain or vanilla)
- 1/4 cup chopped fresh or dried figs
- 1 tablespoon chopped pistachios
- 1/2 teaspoon chia seeds
- 1/4 teaspoon ground cinnamon
- Pinch of nutmeg
- Honey or maple syrup, to taste (optional)

Method:

1. In a jar or container with a lid, combine the rolled oats, milk, yogurt, figs, pistachios, chia seeds, cinnamon, and nutmeg. Stir well to evenly distribute.

2. Cover the jar and refrigerate for at least 8 hours, or overnight, allowing the oats to soften and absorb the flavors.

3. In the morning, stir the mixture one more time. Add honey or maple syrup, if desired, for extra sweetness.

4. Enjoy your chilled overnight oats as is, or garnish with additional chopped figs, pistachios, or a drizzle of nuts and seeds for extra texture and flavor

.

NUTRITIONAL INFORMATION (APPROXIMATE PER SERVING) : Calories: 350, Fat: 10g,

Saturated Fat: 2g, Cholesterol: 15mg, Sodium: 150mg, Carbohydrates: 45g, Fiber: 7g, Sugar: 15g,

Protein: 15g

BREAKFAST BRUSCHETTA WITH AVOCADO & SMOKED SALMON

Prep Time: 10 minutes **Cooking Time**: 5 minutes (optional) **Total Time**: 15 minutes **Servings**: 2

Ingredients:

- 2 slices bread (sourdough, whole wheat, or your favorite)
- 1 tablespoon olive oil
- 1 ripe avocado, halved and pitted
- 1/4 cup thinly sliced smoked salmon
- 1/4 cup cherry tomatoes, halved
- 1 tablespoon chopped fresh dill
- 1 tablespoon lemon juice
- Salt and black pepper to taste
- Optional toppings: crumbled feta cheese, sliced red onion, capers

Method:

1. If desired, brush the bread slices with olive oil and toast until golden brown.
2. Mash the avocado flesh with a fork until slightly chunky. Season with salt and pepper.
3. Spread the mashed avocado onto the toasted bread.
4. Top with the sliced smoked salmon, cherry tomato halves, and chopped dill.
5. Drizzle with lemon juice and a dash of olive oil.
6. Season with additional salt and pepper to taste.
7. Add any optional toppings of your choice, like crumbled feta cheese, sliced red onion, or capers.

NUTRITIONAL INFORMATION (PER SERVING, APPROXIMATE) : Calories: 350, Fat: 20g,

Saturated Fat: 3g, Cholesterol: 50mg, Sodium: 300mg, Carbohydrates: 30g, Fiber: 5g, Sugar: 5g,

Protein: 15g

CHAPTER TWO

LUNCH

11. SPICY SHRIMP SKEWERS WITH COUSCOUS AND TZATZIKI

12. BAKED FALAFEL PITA POCKETS WITH MINT YOGURT SAUCE

13. MEDITERRANEAN FLATBREAD PIZZAS WITH FIG, GOAT CHEESE, AND HONEY

14. SUMMER VEGETABLE PASTA SALAD WITH PESTO AND FETA

15. SALMON AND SPINACH STUFFED PORTOBELLO MUSHROOMS

16. MEDITERRANEAN CHICKEN AND CHICKPEA SALAD SANDWICHES ON WHOLE WHEAT BAGELS

17. GREEK LENTIL SOUP WITH LEMON AND HERBS

18. TUNA MELT WITH WHITE BEANS AND HERBS.

19. MEDITERRANEAN CHICKEN SKEWERS WITH COUSCOUS AND LEMON TAHINI SAUCE

20. GRILLED HALLOUMI SALAD WITH WATERMELON AND MINT

SPICY SHRIMP SKEWERS WITH COUSCOUS AND TZATZIKI

Prep Time: 20 minutes **Cooking Time**: 15 minutes **Total Time**: 35 minutes **Servings**: 4

Ingredients:

- 1 pound large shrimp, peeled and deveined
- 2 tablespoons olive oil
- 1 tablespoon lemon juice
- 1 teaspoon smoked paprika
- 1/2 teaspoon chili powder
- 1/4 teaspoon garlic powder
- 1/4 teaspoon cayenne pepper (adjust to your spice preference)
- Salt and black pepper to taste
- Wooden skewers
- 1 cup Israeli couscous (pearl couscous)
- 1 tablespoon olive oil
- 1 cup vegetable broth
- 1/2 cup chopped red onion
- 1/2 cup chopped cucumber
- 1/4 cup chopped cherry tomatoes
- 1/4 cup chopped fresh parsley
- Salt and black pepper to taste
- 1 cup plain Greek yogurt
- 1/2 cucumber, grated and squeezed to remove excess moisture
- 1 tablespoon chopped fresh dill
- 1 tablespoon olive oil
- 1 clove garlic, minced
- 1/2 teaspoon lemon juice
- Salt and black pepper to taste

Method:

1. Marinate the Shrimp: In a bowl, combine olive oil, lemon juice, paprika, chili powder, garlic powder, cayenne pepper, salt, and pepper. Add the shrimp and toss to coat evenly. Marinate for at least 15 minutes.

2. Cook the Couscous: Heat olive oil in a pot over medium heat. Add the couscous and toast for 1 minute. Pour in the vegetable broth and bring to a boil. Reduce heat, cover, and simmer for 10 minutes, or until the couscous is fluffy and cooked through. Fluff with a fork and set aside.

3. Prepare the Tzatziki: In a bowl, combine the Greek yogurt, grated cucumber, dill, olive oil, garlic, lemon juice, salt, and pepper. Stir well and set aside.

4. Grill the Shrimp: Preheat grill to medium-high heat. Thread the marinated shrimp onto skewers. Grill for 3-4 minutes per side, or until cooked through and pink.

5. Assemble and Serve: Assemble the dish by spooning the couscous onto plates. Top with the shrimp skewers, a dollop of tzatziki, and a sprinkle of fresh parsley. Enjoy!

NUTRITIONAL INFORMATION (PER SERVING, APPROXIMATE):

Calories: 450, Fat: 15gm, Saturated Fat: 3g, Cholesterol: 250mg, Sodium: 500mg, Carbohydrates: 45g, Fiber: 5g, Sugar: 5g, Protein: 30g

BAKED FALAFEL PITA POCKETS WITH MINT YOGURT SAUCE

Prep Time: 15 minutes **Cooking Time**: 20 minutes **Total Time**: 35 minutes **Servings**: 4

Ingredients:

FOR THE FALAFEL:

- 1 can (15 oz) chickpeas, drained and rinsed
- 1/2 onion, finely chopped
- 1/2 cup fresh parsley, chopped
- 1/4 cup fresh cilantro, chopped
- 2 cloves garlic, minced
- 1 teaspoon ground cumin
- 1/2 teaspoon ground coriander
- 1/4 teaspoon turmeric
- 1/4 teaspoon cayenne pepper (adjust to your spice preference)
- Salt and black pepper to taste
- Olive oil for spraying

FOR THE PITA POCKETS:

- 4 pita breads
- Olive oil for drizzling
- For the Mint Yogurt Sauce:
- 1 cup plain Greek yogurt
- 1/4 cup chopped fresh mint
- 1/2 tablespoon lemon juice
- 1 clove garlic, minced
- Salt and black pepper to taste

OPTIONAL TOPPINGS:

- Chopped cucumbers, tomatoes, lettuce, red onion
- Hummus
- Tahini sauce
- Hot sauce

Method:

1. Prepare the Falafel: Preheat oven to 400°F (200°C). In a food processor, pulse the chickpeas, onion, parsley, cilantro, garlic, spices, salt, and pepper until a coarse mixture forms. Don't over-process.

2. Shape the Falafel: Form the mixture into small balls (about 1 inch diameter). If the mixture feels too dry, add a tablespoon of water at a time until it holds its shape.

3. Bake the Falafel: Lightly spray a baking sheet with olive oil. Arrange the falafel balls on the sheet and spray them with olive oil. Bake for 20 minutes, flipping halfway through, until golden brown and crispy.

4. Warm the Pita Breads: Drizzle each pita bread with olive oil and lightly toast in the oven or on a pan for a few minutes until warmed through.

5. Make the Mint Yogurt Sauce: In a bowl, combine the Greek yogurt, mint, lemon juice, garlic, salt, and pepper. Stir well and set aside.

6. Assemble the Pita Pockets: Fill each pita bread with warm falafel balls. Drizzle with mint yogurt sauce and add any desired toppings. Serve immediately and enjoy!

NUTRITIONAL INFORMATION (PER SERVING, APPROXIMATE) :

Calories: 400, Fat: 15g, Saturated Fat: 2g, Cholesterol: 0mg, Sodium: 350mg, Carbohydrates: 45g, Fiber: 8g, Sugar: 5g, Protein: 15g

MEDITERRANEAN FLATBREAD PIZZAS WITH FIG, GOAT CHEESE, AND HONEY

Prep Time: 10 minutes **Cooking Time**: 15 minutes **Total Time**: 25 minutes **Servings:** 4 (2 pizzas each)

Ingredients:

- 2 whole wheat flatbreads
- 2 tablespoons olive oil
- 1 cup fresh figs, thinly sliced
- 4 ounces goat cheese, crumbled

- 1/4 cup chopped fresh rosemary or thyme (optional)
- 1 tablespoon honey
- Salt and black pepper to taste

Method:

1. Preheat oven to 400°F (200°C).
2. Brush each flatbread with olive oil. Arrange the fig slices evenly on top.
3. Crumble the goat cheese over the figs, leaving some space in the center. Sprinkle with rosemary or thyme, if using.
4. Bake for 10-12 minutes, until the edges of the flatbreads are golden brown and the cheese is slightly melted.
5. Drizzle each pizza with honey and season with salt and pepper to taste.
6. Cut each flatbread in half and serve immediately.

NUTRITIONAL INFORMATION (PER SERVING, APPROXIMATE) : Calories: 300, Fat: 15g, Saturated Fat: 3g, Cholesterol: 15mg, Sodium: 300mg, Carbohydrates: 30g, Fiber: 5g, Sugar: 20g, Protein: 8g

Prep Time: 15 minutes **Cooking Time:** 10 minutes **Total Time:** 25 minutes **Servings:** 4-6

Ingredients:

- 1 pound pasta (fusilli, farfalle, penne, or your favorite shape)
- 1/2 cup homemade or store-bought pesto
- 1/4 cup crumbled feta cheese
- 1 cup cherry tomatoes, halved
- 1/2 cup chopped cucumber

- 1/2 cup chopped zucchini
- 1/4 cup red onion, thinly sliced
- 1/4 cup chopped fresh basil
- 2 tablespoons olive oil
- Salt and black pepper to taste

OPTIONAL ADDITIONS:

- 1/2 cup cooked chickpeas or corn
- Kalamata olives, chopped

- Grilled chicken or shrimp, sliced
- Balsamic vinegar glaze, for drizzling

Method:

1. Cook the pasta according to package instructions until al dente. Drain and rinse under cold water to stop the cooking process.
2. In a large bowl, combine the cooked pasta, pesto, and feta cheese. Toss to coat evenly.
3. Add the cherry tomatoes, cucumber, zucchini, red onion, and basil. Drizzle with olive oil and season with salt and pepper to taste.
4. Gently toss to combine all the ingredients.
5. Serve immediately at room temperature, or chill for at least 30 minutes for enhanced flavors.

NUTRITIONAL INFORMATION (PER SERVING, APPROXIMATE) : Calories: 450, Fat: 15g, Saturated Fat: 3g, Cholesterol: 5mg, Sodium: 350mg, Carbohydrates: 45g, Fiber: 5g, Sugar: 5g, Protein: 15g

SALMON AND SPINACH STUFFED PORTOBELLO MUSHROOMS

Prep Time: 15 minutes **Cooking Time**: 25 minutes **Total Time**: 40 minutes **Servings**: 4

Ingredients:

- 4 large portobello mushrooms
- 1 tablespoon olive oil
- Salt and black pepper to taste
- 1 tablespoon lemon juice
- 1 red onion, finely chopped
- 2 cloves garlic, minced
- Optional toppings: cherry tomatoes, fresh herbs, lemon wedges

- 4 ounces fresh spinach, chopped
- 12 ounces salmon fillet, cooked and flaked
- 1/4 cup ricotta cheese
- 1/4 cup grated Parmesan cheese
- 1/4 cup chopped fresh parsley

Method:

1. Preheat oven to 400°F (200°C).
2. Gently clean the portobello mushrooms with a damp paper towel. Remove the stems and gently scrape out the gills without damaging the caps. Drizzle with olive oil and season with salt and pepper.
3. Brush the inside of the mushrooms with lemon juice.
4. Heat a tablespoon of olive oil in a pan over medium heat. Add the chopped onion and cook until softened, about 5 minutes. Add the garlic and cook for another minute until fragrant.
5. Add the chopped spinach and cook until wilted. Remove from heat and let cool slightly.
6. In a bowl, combine the flaked salmon, ricotta cheese, Parmesan cheese, parsley, cooled spinach mixture, and additional salt and pepper to taste.
7. Divide the salmon mixture evenly among the portobello mushroom caps.
8. Place the stuffed mushrooms on a baking sheet and bake for 20-25 minutes, or until the filling is hot and bubbly.
9. Serve immediately, garnished with optional cherry tomatoes, fresh herbs, and lemon wedges, if desired.

NUTRITIONAL INFORMATION (PER SERVING, APPROXIMATE):

Calories: 450, Fat: 20g, Saturated Fat: 5g, Cholesterol: 100mg, Sodium: 500mg

Carbohydrates: 20g, Fiber: 3g, Sugar: 5g, Protein: 35g

NUTRITIONAL INFORMATION (PER SERVING, APPROXIMATE):

MEDITERRANEAN CHICKEN AND CHICKPEA SALAD SANDWICHES ON WHOLE WHEAT BAGELS

Prep Time: 15 minutes **Cooking Time**: 20 minutes **Total Time**: 35 minutes **Servings:** 2

Ingredients:

FOR THE CHICKEN SALAD:

- 1 boneless, skinless chicken breast (cooked and shredded)
- 1 can (15 oz) chickpeas, drained and rinsed
- 1/2 cup chopped cucumber
- 1/4 cup chopped red onion
- 1/4 cup chopped cherry tomatoes
- 1/4 cup chopped Kalamata olives
- 2 tablespoons chopped fresh parsley
- 1 tablespoon olive oil
- 1 tablespoon lemon juice
- 1/2 cup plain Greek yogurt
- 1/2 teaspoon dried oregano
- Salt and black pepper to taste
- For the Sandwiches:
- 2 whole wheat bagels, toasted and sliced in half
- Optional toppings: lettuce, sliced avocado, hummus

Method:

1. In a large bowl, combine the shredded chicken, chickpeas, cucumber, red onion, cherry tomatoes, Kalamata olives, and parsley.
2. In a separate bowl, whisk together the olive oil, lemon juice, Greek yogurt, oregano, salt, and pepper.
3. Pour the dressing over the chicken and chickpea mixture and toss to coat evenly.
4. Toast the whole wheat bagels and assemble the sandwiches with the desired amount of chicken salad.
5. Add optional toppings like lettuce, sliced avocado, or hummus for extra flavor and texture.
6. Enjoy your sunshine-filled Mediterranean chicken salad sandwich

NUTRITIONAL INFORMATION (PER SERVING, APPROXIMATE): Calories: 450Fat: 15g, Saturated Fat: 3g, Cholesterol: 50mg, Sodium: 500mg, Carbohydrates: 40g, Fiber: 5g, Sugar: 5g, Protein: 30g

GREEK LENTIL SOUP WITH LEMON AND HERBS

Prep Time: 15 minutes **Cooking Time**: 30 minutes **Total Time**: 45 minutes **Servings**: 4-6

Ingredients:

- 1 tablespoon olive oil
- 1 onion, chopped
- 2 cloves garlic, minced
- 1 cup brown lentils, rinsed
- 4 cups vegetable broth
- Salt and black pepper to taste

- 1 (14.5 oz) can diced tomatoes, undrained
- 1/2 cup chopped fresh parsley
- 1/4 cup chopped fresh mint
- 1/4 cup chopped fresh dill
- 1 tablespoon lemon juice
- Optional toppings: crumbled feta cheese, chopped fresh olives, crusty bread

Method:

1. Heat olive oil in a large pot over medium heat. Add the chopped onion and cook until softened, about 5 minutes.
2. Add the minced garlic and cook for another minute until fragrant.
3. Stir in the rinsed lentils, vegetable broth, and diced tomatoes (with their juices). Bring to a boil, then reduce heat and simmer for 20-25 minutes, or until the lentils are tender.
4. While the soup simmers, chop the parsley, mint, and dill.
5. Once the lentils are cooked, stir in the chopped herbs and lemon juice. Season with salt and pepper to taste.
6. Ladle the hot soup into bowls and garnish with crumbled feta cheese, chopped olives, and a crusty bread slice, if desired.

NUTRITIONAL INFORMATION (PER SERVING, APPROXIMATE):

Calories: 300, Fat: 5g, Saturated Fat: 1g, Cholesterol: 0mg, Sodium: 350mg, Carbohydrates: 40g

Fiber: 8g, Sugar: 5g, Protein: 15g

Prep Time: 10 minutes **Cooking Time:** 5 minutes **Total Time**: 15 minutes **Servings:** 2

Ingredients:

- 2 cans (5 oz each) tuna, drained and flaked
- 1 can (15 oz) cannellini beans, drained and rinsed
- 1/4 cup chopped celery
- 1/4 cup chopped red onion
- 2 tablespoons chopped fresh dill
- 2 tablespoons chopped fresh parsley
- 1 tablespoon lemon juice
- 1 tablespoon mayonnaise (can substitute Greek yogurt or vegan mayo)
- 1/2 teaspoon Dijon mustard
- Salt and black pepper to taste
- 2 whole wheat bread slices
- Optional toppings: sliced avocado, tomato, sprouts, lettuce

Method:

1. In a bowl, combine the flaked tuna, cannellini beans, celery, red onion, dill, parsley, lemon juice, mayonnaise, Dijon mustard, salt, and pepper. Mix well to combine.
2. Toast the bread slices to your desired level of crispness.
3. Spread the tuna mixture onto the toasted bread slices. Add any desired toppings like avocado, tomato, sprouts, or lettuce.
4. Cut the sandwiches in half and enjoy!

NUTRITIONAL INFORMATION (PER SERVING, APPROXIMATE) :

Calories: 400, Fat: 15g, Saturated Fat: 3g, Cholesterol: 50mg, Sodium: 400mg, Carbohydrates: 40g, Fiber: 8g, Sugar: 5g, Protein: 30g

MEDITERRANEAN CHICKEN SKEWERS WITH COUSCOUS AND LEMON TAHINI SAUCE

Prep Time: 20 minutes Cooking Time: 15 minutes **Total Time**: 35 minutes **Servings**: 4

Ingredients:

FOR THE CHICKEN SKEWERS:

- 1 pound boneless, skinless chicken breasts, cut into bite-sized pieces
- 2 tablespoons olive oil
- 1 tablespoon lemon juice
- 1 teaspoon paprika
- 1/2 teaspoon cumin

- 1/2 teaspoon garlic powder
- 1/4 teaspoon cayenne pepper (adjust to your spice preference)
- Salt and black pepper to taste
- Wooden skewers

FOR THE COUSCOUS:

1. 1 cup Israeli couscous (pearl couscous)
2. 1 tablespoon olive oil
3. 1 cup vegetable broth
4. 1/2 cup chopped red onion
5. 1/2 cup chopped cucumber
6. 1/4 cup chopped cherry tomatoes
7. 1/4 cup chopped fresh parsley
8. Salt and black pepper to taste

9. For the Lemon Tahini Sauce:
10. 1 cup plain Greek yogurt
11. 1/4 cup tahini (sesame seed paste)
12. 2 tablespoons lemon juice
13. 1 clove garlic, minced
14. 1/4 cup water
15. Salt and black pepper to taste

Method:

1. Marinate the Chicken: In a bowl, combine olive oil, lemon juice, paprika, cumin, garlic powder, cayenne pepper, salt, and pepper. Add the chicken pieces and toss to coat evenly. Marinate for at least 15 minutes.

2. Cook the Couscous: Heat olive oil in a pot over medium heat. Add the couscous and toast for 1 minute. Pour in the vegetable broth and bring to a boil. Reduce heat, cover, and simmer for 10 minutes, or until the couscous is fluffy and cooked through. Fluff with a fork and set aside.

3. Prepare the Tahini Sauce: In a bowl, whisk together the Greek yogurt, tahini, lemon juice, garlic, water, salt, and pepper.

4. Grill the Chicken: Preheat grill to medium-high heat. Thread the marinated chicken onto skewers. Grill for 3-4 minutes per side, or until cooked through and golden brown.

5. Assemble and Serve: Assemble the dish by spooning the couscous onto plates. Top with the grilled chicken skewers, a dollop of lemon tahini sauce, and a sprinkle of fresh parsley. Enjoy!

NUTRITIONAL INFORMATION (PER SERVING, APPROXIMATE) : Calories: 450, Fat: 15g,

Saturated Fat: 3g, Cholesterol: 50mg, Sodium: 500mg, Carbohydrates: 45g, Fiber: 5g, Sugar: 5g,

Protein: 30g

GRILLED HALLOUMI SALAD WITH WATERMELON AND MINT

Prep Time: 15 minutes **Cooking Time**: 10 minutes **Total Time**: 25 minutes **Servings**: 4

Ingredients:

- 1 pound seedless watermelon, cut into 1-inch cubes
- 12 ounces halloumi cheese, sliced 1/2 inch thick
- 1/4 cup olive oil
- 2 tablespoons lemon juice
- 1 tablespoon chopped fresh mint
- 1/2 teaspoon honey
- Salt and black pepper to taste
- Optional toppings: crumbled feta cheese, chopped red onion, balsamic glaze, fresh herbs

Method:

- Preheat grill or grill pan to medium-high heat. Lightly brush the halloumi slices with olive oil and season with salt and pepper.
- In a small bowl, whisk together olive oil, lemon juice, mint, honey, salt, and pepper.
- Grill the halloumi slices for 2-3 minutes per side, or until golden brown and slightly crispy.
- In a large bowl, toss the watermelon cubes with half of the dressing.
- Arrange the dressed watermelon on a serving platter. Top with the grilled halloumi slices and drizzle with the remaining dressing.
- Garnish with crumbled feta cheese, chopped red onion, balsamic glaze, and fresh herbs, if desired.

NUTRITIONAL INFORMATION (PER SERVING, APPROXIMATE):

Calories: 250, Fat: 10g, Saturated Fat: 5g, Cholesterol: 30mg, Sodium: 300mg, Carbohydrates: 30g

Fiber: 2g, Sugar: 25g, Protein: 10g

CHAPHER THREE

DINNER

21. SEAFOOD PAELLA WITH SAFFRON AND ROSEMARY:

22. SLOW-COOKER MOROCCAN CHICKEN TAGINE WITH PRUNES AND ALMONDS FEAST.

23. ROASTED EGGPLANT MOUSSAKA WITH BÉCHAMEL SAUCE

24. PESTO-CRUSTED SALMON WITH SUN-DRIED TOMATOES AND CAPERS

25. LAMB KEBABS WITH LEMON & OREGANO, GRILLED VEGETABLES & TZATZIKI

26. ONE-PAN LEMON THYME CHICKEN WITH ROASTED RADISHES & POTATOES

27. ROASTED COD WITH FENNEL & OLIVES

28. SPICED CHICKPEA TAGINE WITH SWEET POTATO AND SPINACH.

29. GREEK SHRIMP SAGANAKI WITH FETA AND TOMATOES

30. GRILLED HALLOUMI SALAD WITH WATERMELON AND MINT

SEAFOOD PAELLA WITH SAFFRON AND ROSEMARY:

Prep Time: 20 minutes **Cooking Time**: 40 minutes **Total Time**: 60 minutes **Servings**: 4-6

Ingredients:

- 1/4 cup olive oil
- 1 large onion, chopped
- 3 cloves garlic, minced
- 1 red bell pepper, chopped
- 1 green bell pepper, chopped
- 1 cup bomba rice (or short-grain rice)
- 1 teaspoon smoked paprika
- 1/2 teaspoon ground turmeric
- Pinch of saffron threads

- 5 cups fish broth (or seafood stock)
- 1 pound mussels, debearded and rinsed
- 1 pound raw shrimp, peeled and deveined
- 1/2 pound scallops
- 1/4 cup chopped fresh parsley
- 1/4 cup chopped fresh rosemary
- Salt and black pepper to taste
- Lemon wedges, for serving (optional)

Method:

1. Heat olive oil in a large paella pan or Dutch oven over medium heat. Add the onion and cook until softened, about 5 minutes.
2. Stir in the garlic and bell peppers, and cook for another 5 minutes.
3. Add the rice and stir to coat with the oil and vegetables. Toast the rice for 1 minute.
4. Stir in the paprika, turmeric, and saffron threads.
5. Pour in the fish broth and bring to a boil. Reduce heat to low, cover, and simmer for 20 minutes, or until the rice is almost cooked through.
6. Nestle the mussels and shrimp into the rice. Scatter the scallops on top. Cover and cook for an additional 5-7 minutes, or until the mussels have opened and the shrimp and scallops are cooked through.
7. Turn off the heat and let the paella stand for 5 minutes before serving.
8. Sprinkle with chopped parsley and rosemary. Season with salt and pepper to taste.
9. Serve hot with lemon wedges, if desired.

NUTRITIONAL INFORMATION (PER SERVING, APPROXIMATE):

Calories: 500, Fat: 20g, Saturated Fat: 3g, Cholesterol: 250mg, Sodium: 500mg

Carbohydrates: 60g, Fiber: 2g, Sugar: 5g, Protein: 40g

SLOW-COOKER MOROCCAN CHICKEN TAGINE WITH PRUNES AND ALMONDS FEAST.

Prep Time: 15 minutes **Cooking Time**: 7-8 hours on low (or 4-5 hours on high) **Total Time**: 7-8 hours 15 minutes (or 4-5 hours 15 minutes) **Servings**: 4-6

Ingredients:

- 1 tablespoon olive oil
- 1 large onion, chopped
- 2 cloves garlic, minced
- 1 teaspoon ground ginger
- 1 teaspoon ground cinnamon
- 1/2 teaspoon turmeric
- 1/4 teaspoon ground cumin
- 1/4 teaspoon cayenne pepper (adjust to your spice preference)

- Salt and black pepper to taste
- 1 (3-4 pound) whole chicken, cut into 8 pieces
- 1/2 cup pitted prunes
- 1/2 cup blanched whole almonds
- 1 cup chicken broth
- 1/4 cup chopped fresh cilantro, for garnish (optional)

Method:

1. Heat olive oil in a large skillet over medium heat. Add the onion and cook until softened, about 5 minutes.
2. Stir in the garlic, ginger, cinnamon, turmeric, cumin, cayenne pepper, salt, and pepper. Cook for an additional minute, until fragrant.
3. Transfer the onion mixture to the slow cooker.
4. Season the chicken pieces with salt and pepper. Arrange them in a single layer over the onion mixture.
5. Scatter the prunes and almonds around the chicken.
6. Pour the chicken broth into the slow cooker.
7. Cover and cook on low for 7-8 hours, or on high for 4-5 hours, or until the chicken is tender and falling off the bone.
8. Garnish with fresh cilantro, if desired.
9. Serve the tagine hot with couscous or rice

NUTRITIONAL INFORMATION (PER SERVING, APPROXIMATE) :

Calories: 500, Fat: 20g, Saturated Fat: 3g, Cholesterol: 100mg, Sodium: 500mg, Carbohydrates: 40g

Fiber: 5g, Sugar: 20g, Protein: 40g

ROASTED EGGPLANT MOUSSAKA WITH BéCHAMEL SAUCE

Prep Time: 20 minutes **Cooking Time:** 1 hour 15 minutes **Total Time:** 1 hour 35 minutes **Servings**: 4-6

Ingredients:

FOR THE EGGPLANT:

- 2 large eggplants
- 2 tablespoons olive oil
- Salt and black pepper to taste
- For the Meat Sauce:
- 1 tablespoon olive oil
- 1 large onion, chopped
- 2 cloves garlic, minced

- 1 pound ground lamb or beef
- 1 (28 oz) can crushed tomatoes
- 1 teaspoon dried oregano
- 1/2 teaspoon ground cinnamon
- 1/4 teaspoon ground nutmeg
- Salt and black pepper to taste

FOR THE BéCHAMEL SAUCE:

- 3 tablespoons butter
- 3 tablespoons all-purpose flour
- 2 cups milk, warmed

- 1/4 teaspoon ground nutmeg
- Salt and black pepper to taste
- 1/2 cup grated Parmesan cheese

FOR ASSEMBLY:

- 1/4 cup breadcrumbs

Method:

1. Preheat oven to 400°F (200°C).

2. Prepare the Eggplant: Slice the eggplants lengthwise into ½-inch thick sheets. Liberally sprinkle with salt and let sit for 30 minutes to draw out excess moisture. Pat dry with paper towels. Brush both sides of the eggplant slices with olive oil and season with salt and pepper. Place on a baking sheet and roast for 20-25 minutes, or until tender and lightly browned.

3. Make the Meat Sauce: Heat olive oil in a large skillet over medium heat. Add the onion and cook until softened, about 5 minutes. Stir in the garlic and cook for another minute until fragrant.

4. Add the ground lamb or beef and cook until browned, breaking it up with a spoon. Drain any excess fat.

5. Stir in the crushed tomatoes, oregano, cinnamon, nutmeg, salt, and pepper. Bring to a simmer and cook for 15 minutes, or until the sauce thickens slightly.

6. Make the Béchamel Sauce: In a saucepan, melt the butter over medium heat. Whisk in the flour and cook for 1 minute, stirring constantly.

7. Slowly whisk in the warmed milk until smooth. Bring to a simmer and cook for 5 minutes, whisking constantly, until thickened and creamy. Stir in the nutmeg, salt, and pepper.

8. Assemble the Moussaka: Spread half of the meat sauce in the bottom of a greased baking dish. Layer with half of the roasted eggplant slices and sprinkle with half of the breadcrumbs. Repeat with the remaining meat sauce, eggplant, and breadcrumbs.

9. Pour the béchamel sauce over the top, spreading evenly. Sprinkle with the grated Parmesan cheese.

10. Bake for 25-30 minutes, or until golden brown and bubbly. Let cool for 10 minutes before serving.

NUTRITIONAL INFORMATION (PER SERVING, APPROXIMATE):

Calories: 550, Fat: 25g, Saturated Fat: 10g, Cholesterol: 100mg, Sodium: 700mg, Carbohydrates: 50g, Fiber: 5g, Sugar: 10g, Protein: 35g

PESTO- CRUSTED SALMON WITH SUN- DRIED TOMATOES AND CAPERS

Prep Time: 15 minutes **Cooking Time**: 15-20 minutes **Total Time**: 30-35 minutes **Servings**: 2-3

Ingredients:

- 2-3 salmon fillets (each about 6 oz)
- 1/4 cup store-bought pesto or homemade pesto
- 1/4 cup sun-dried tomatoes, finely chopped
- 1 tablespoon capers, drained

- 1 tablespoon olive oil
- Salt and black pepper to taste
- Garnish: Fresh basil leaves, lemon wedges (optional)

Method:

1. Preheat oven to 400°F (200°C). Line a baking sheet with parchment paper.
2. Season the salmon: Pat the salmon fillets dry with paper towels. Season both sides with salt and pepper.
3. Spread the pesto: Spread a thin layer of pesto evenly over the top of each salmon fillet.
4. Top with sun-dried tomatoes and capers: Sprinkle the chopped sun-dried tomatoes and drained capers over the pesto-coated salmon.
5. Drizzle with olive oil: Drizzle a little olive oil over the salmon to add moisture and sheen.
6. Bake: Bake the salmon for 15-20 minutes, or until cooked through and flaky. The internal temperature should reach 145°F (63°C).
7. Garnish and serve: Garnish with fresh basil leaves and lemon wedges, if desired. Serve immediately with your favorite sides like roasted vegetables, rice, or couscous.

NUTRITIONAL INFORMATION (PER SERVING, APPROXIMATE) :

Calories: 450, Fat: 25g, Saturated Fat: 5g, Cholesterol: 80mg, Sodium: 500mg, Carbohydrates: 5g, Fiber: 1g, Sugar: 5g, Protein: 40g

Prep Time: 20 minutes (plus marinating time) **Cooking Time**: 15-20 minutes **Total Time**: 35-45 minutes (depending on marinating time) **Servings**: 4-6

Ingredients:

FOR THE LAMB KEBABS:

- 1 pound boneless, skinless lamb shoulder, cut into 1-inch cubes
- 1/4 cup olive oil
- 2 tablespoons lemon juice
- 1 tablespoon chopped fresh oregano
- 1 teaspoon garlic powder
- 1/2 teaspoon salt
- 1/4 teaspoon black pepper
- Wooden skewers

FOR THE GRILLED VEGETABLES:

- 1 red bell pepper, sliced
- 1 green bell pepper, sliced
- 1 red onion, sliced
- 1 zucchini, sliced
- 1 tablespoon olive oil
- Salt and black pepper to taste
- For the Tzatziki Sauce:
- 1 cup plain Greek yogurt
- 1/2 cucumber, seeded and grated
- 1 clove garlic, minced
- 1 tablespoon fresh dill, chopped
- 1 tablespoon lemon juice
- Salt and black pepper to taste

Method:

- Marinate the Lamb: In a bowl, combine olive oil, lemon juice, oregano, garlic powder, salt, and pepper. Add the lamb cubes and toss to coat evenly. Cover and refrigerate for at least 1 hour, or up to overnight for richer flavor.

- Prepare the Vegetables: Slice the bell peppers, onion, and zucchini. Toss with olive oil, salt, and pepper.
- Make the Tzatziki Sauce: Grate the cucumber and squeeze out excess moisture. In a bowl, combine Greek yogurt, cucumber, garlic, dill, lemon juice, salt, and pepper. Mix well and refrigerate until serving.
- Prepare the Grill: Preheat grill to medium-high heat.
- Thread the Kebabs: Thread the marinated lamb cubes onto skewers.
- Grill the Kebabs and Vegetables: Grill the lamb skewers for 3-4 minutes per side, or until cooked through to your desired doneness. Grill the vegetables for 2-3 minutes per side, or until tender-crisp.
- Assemble and Serve: Serve the lamb kebabs and grilled vegetables on a platter with a dollop of tzatziki sauce.

NUTRITIONAL INFORMATION (PER SERVING, APPROXIMATE):

Calories: 450, Fat: 20g, Saturated Fat: 5g, Cholesterol: 100mg, Sodium: 400mg, Carbohydrates: 30g, Fiber: 5g, Sugar: 5g, Protein: 40g

Prep Time: 15 minutes **Cooking Time**: 45-50 minutes **Total Time**: 60 minutes **Servings**: 4

Ingredients:

- 1 whole chicken, cut into 8 pieces (or 4 bone-in, skin-on chicken thighs)
- 1 tablespoon olive oil
- 1 lemon, zested and juiced
- 1 tablespoon chopped fresh thyme
- 1 teaspoon garlic powder
- 1/2 teaspoon salt
- 1/4 teaspoon black pepper
- 1 pound small radishes, trimmed and halved
- 1 pound baby potatoes, halved
- 1/4 cup chopped fresh parsley, for garnish (optional)

Method:

- Preheat oven to 425°F (220°C).
- In a large bowl, toss the chicken pieces with olive oil, lemon zest, lemon juice, thyme, garlic powder, salt, and pepper.
- Add the radishes and potatoes to the bowl and toss to coat with the chicken marinade.
- Spread the chicken and vegetables in a single layer on a large rimmed baking sheet.
- Roast for 45-50 minutes, or until the chicken is cooked through and the vegetables are tender and golden brown, flipping the chicken halfway through cooking.
- Garnish with chopped parsley, if desired.
- Serve immediately with your favorite sides like roasted asparagus, green beans, or couscous.

NUTRITIONAL INFORMATION (PER SERVING, APPROXIMATE) : Calories: 550, Fat: 25g, ,

Saturated Fat: 5g, Cholesterol: 130mg, Sodium: 500mg, Carbohydrates: 45g, Fiber: 5g, Sugar: 5g,

Protein: 40g

ROASTED COD WITH FENNEL & OLIVES

Prep Time: 15 minutes **Cooking Time**: 20-25 minutes **Total Time**: 35-40 minutes **Servings: 4**

Ingredients:

- 1 pound cod fillets, cut into 4 equal pieces
- 1 tablespoon olive oil
- 1/2 teaspoon salt
- 1/4 teaspoon black pepper
- 1 large fennel bulb, thinly sliced
- 1/2 cup kalamata olives, pitted and halved
- 1/4 cup cherry tomatoes, halved (optional)
- 1 lemon, sliced
- 2 tablespoons chopped fresh parsley, for garnish
- Lemon wedges, for serving (optional)

Method:

1. Preheat oven to 400°F (200°C).
2. In a small bowl, toss the cod fillets with olive oil, salt, and pepper.
3. Spread the fennel slices in a single layer on a large baking sheet. Arrange the cod pieces on top. Scatter the olives and cherry tomatoes around the cod, if using.
4. Top with lemon slices.
5. Roast for 20-25 minutes, or until the cod is opaque and flakes easily with a fork and the fennel is tender-crisp.
6. Garnish with chopped parsley and serve immediately with lemon wedges, if desired.

NUTRITIONAL INFORMATION (PER SERVING, APPROXIMATE) : Calories: 350, Fat: 15g,

Saturated Fat: 2g, Cholesterol: 80mg, Sodium: 350mg, Carbohydrates: 15g, Fiber: 3g, Sugar: 5g,

Protein: 35g

SPICED CHICKPEA TAGINE WITH SWEET POTATO AND SPINACH.

Prep Time: 15 minutes **Cooking Time**: 40 minutes **Total Time**: 55 minutes **Servings**: 4-6

Ingredients:

- 1 tablespoon olive oil
- 1 large onion, chopped
- 2 cloves garlic, minced
- 1 teaspoon ground cumin
- 1 teaspoon ground coriander
- 1/2 teaspoon turmeric
- 1/4 teaspoon ground cinnamon
- 1/4 teaspoon ground ginger
- 1/4 teaspoon chili flakes (adjust to your spice preference)
- 1 (14.5 oz) can diced tomatoes, undrained
- 1 cup vegetable broth
- 1 (15 oz) can chickpeas, drained and rinsed
- 1 large sweet potato, peeled and cubed
- 5 oz baby spinach
- 1/4 cup chopped fresh cilantro, for garnish (optional)
- Couscous or rice, for serving

Method:

1. Heat olive oil in a large Dutch oven or pot over medium heat. Add the onion and cook until softened, about 5 minutes.
2. Stir in the garlic, cumin, coriander, turmeric, cinnamon, ginger, and chili flakes. Cook for an additional minute, until fragrant.
3. Add the diced tomatoes, vegetable broth, chickpeas, and sweet potato. Bring to a simmer, cover, and cook for 20 minutes, or until the sweet potato is tender.
4. Stir in the spinach and cook for 1-2 minutes, or until wilted.
5. Season with salt and pepper to taste.
6. Garnish with chopped cilantro, if desired.
7. Serve hot with couscous or rice

NUTRITIONAL INFORMATION (PER SERVING, APPROXIMATE): Calories: 350, Fat: 10g, Saturated Fat: 1g, Cholesterol: 0mg, Sodium: 350mg, Carbohydrates: 50g, Fiber: 10g, Sugar: 10g, Protein: 15g

GREEK SHRIMP SAGANAKI WITH FETA AND TOMATOES

Prep Time: 15 minutes **Cooking Time**: 20-25 minutes **Total Time**: 35-40 minutes **Servings**: 4

Ingredients:

- 1 tablespoon olive oil
- 1 large onion, chopped
- 2 cloves garlic, minced
- 1 (28 oz) can diced tomatoes, undrained
- 1/2 cup crumbled feta cheese
- 1/4 teaspoon dried oregano

- Pinch of red pepper flakes (optional)
- Salt and black pepper to taste
- 1 pound large shrimp, peeled and deveined
- 1/4 cup chopped fresh parsley, for garnish (optional)
- Crusty bread, for serving

1. **Method:**
2. Preheat oven to 400°F (200°C).
3. Heat olive oil in a large oven-proof skillet or casserole dish over medium heat. Add the onion and cook until softened, about 5 minutes.
4. Stir in the garlic and cook for an additional minute until fragrant.
5. Add the diced tomatoes, feta cheese, oregano, and red pepper flakes (if using). Season with salt and pepper to taste. Bring to a simmer and cook for 5 minutes.
6. Nestle the shrimp into the tomato sauce, ensuring they are covered.
7. Transfer the skillet to the preheated oven and bake for 15-20 minutes, or until the shrimp are pink and cooked through.
8. Garnish with chopped parsley, if desired.
9. Serve hot with crusty bread for soaking up the flavorful sauce.

Nutritional Information (per serving, approximate): Calories: 400, Fat: 15g, Saturated Fat: 5g,,, Cholesterol: 200mg, Sodium: 500mg, Carbohydrates: 25g, Fiber: 2g, Sugar: 5g, Protein: 35g

GRILLED HALLOUMI SALAD WITH WATERMELON AND MINT

Prep Time: 10 minutes **Cooking Time**: 10 minutes **Total Time**: 20 minutes **Servings**: 4

Ingredients:

- 1 tablespoon olive oil
- 1/2 red onion, thinly sliced
- 1 cup cherry tomatoes, halved
- 1 pound seedless watermelon, cut into 1-inch cubes
- 1/2 block halloumi cheese, sliced 1/2-inch thick
- 1/4 cup chopped fresh mint
- 2 tablespoons balsamic vinegar
- 1 tablespoon lemon juice
- Salt and black pepper to taste
- Feta cheese crumbles, for garnish (optional)
- Fresh basil leaves, for garnish (optional)

Method:

- Preheat a grill pan or skillet over medium-high heat. Brush the pan with olive oil.
- Grill the red onion slices for 2-3 minutes per side, or until softened and slightly charred.
- Transfer the onion to a bowl.
- Add the cherry tomatoes and watermelon to the bowl.
- In the same pan, grill the halloumi slices for 2-3 minutes per side, or until golden brown and slightly crispy.
- Add the halloumi to the bowl with the vegetables.
- Toss in the chopped mint.
- In a small bowl, whisk together the balsamic vinegar, lemon juice, salt, and pepper. Drizzle the dressing over the salad.
- Garnish with crumbled feta cheese and fresh basil leaves, if desired.
- Serve immediately.

NUTRITIONAL INFORMATION (PER SERVING, APPROXIMATE): Calories: 300, Fat: 15g, Saturated Fat: 5g, Cholesterol: 100mg, Sodium: 300mg, Carbohydrates: 30g, Fiber: 3g, Sugar: 20g, Protein: 10g

CHAPTER FOUR

FRESH SALADS AND APPETIZERS

41. **SPICED LENTIL & QUINOA SALAD WITH ROASTED VEGETABLES**

42. **FATTOUSH SALAD WITH CRISPY PITA BREAD & HERBS**

43. **GREEK SHRIMP SKEWERS WITH TZATZIKI DIP**

44. **MEDITERRANEAN STUFFED PORTOBELLO MUSHROOMS WITH GOAT CHEESE & HERBS.**

45. **SPICY CHICKPEA & MANGO FRITTERS WITH MINT YOGURT DIP.**

46. **WATERMELON & FETA SKEWERS WITH BALSAMIC GLAZE:**

47. **LENTIL & WALNUT PATTIES WITH LEMON TAHINI SAUCE.**

48. **ROASTED PEPPER & ARTICHOKE BRUSCHETTA WITH GOAT CHEESE**

49. **CRISPY HALLOUMI & FIG SALAD WITH HONEY & MINT**

50. **WHITE BEAN & TUNA SALAD BOATS WITH TOASTED PITA BREAD**

SPICED LENTIL & QUINOA SALAD WITH ROASTED VEGETABLES

Prep Time: 15 minutes **Cooking Time**: 45-50 minutes **Total Time**: 60 minutes **Servings**: 6-8

Ingredients:

FOR THE SALAD:

- 1 cup dry brown lentils, rinsed
- 1 cup quinoa, rinsed
- 2 tablespoons olive oil
- 1/2 teaspoon ground cumin

- 1/2 teaspoon ground coriander
- 1/4 teaspoon turmeric
- Pinch of cayenne pepper (optional)
- Salt and black pepper to taste

FOR THE ROASTED VEGETABLES:

- 1 red bell pepper, sliced
- 1 yellow bell pepper, sliced
- 1 red onion, wedges
- 1 zucchini, sliced
- 1 large sweet potato, diced
- 1 tablespoon olive oil
- 1/2 teaspoon dried oregano

- Salt and black pepper to taste
- For the Dressing:
- 3 tablespoons lemon juice
- 2 tablespoons olive oil
- 1 teaspoon honey
- 1/2 teaspoon Dijon mustard
- 1/4 cup chopped fresh parsley

OPTIONAL GARNISHES:

- Chopped fresh cilantro
- Toasted pumpkin seeds

- Crumbled feta cheese

Method:

1. Preheat oven to 425°F (220°C).
2. Cook the lentils and quinoa: Combine lentils, quinoa, 2 tablespoons olive oil, cumin, coriander, turmeric, cayenne pepper (if using), salt, and pepper in a pot. Add 2 cups water and bring to a boil.

Reduce heat, cover, and simmer for 20-25 minutes, or until the lentils are tender and the quinoa is fluffy. Fluff with a fork and set aside to cool slightly.

3. Roast the vegetables: Toss the bell peppers, onion, zucchini, and sweet potato with olive oil, oregano, salt, and pepper. Spread on a large baking sheet and roast for 20-25 minutes, or until tender and slightly browned.

4. Make the dressing: Whisk together lemon juice, olive oil, honey, Dijon mustard, and parsley in a small bowl.

5. Assemble the salad: In a large bowl, combine the cooled lentils and quinoa, roasted vegetables, and dressing. Toss to coat.

6. Garnish with chopped cilantro, toasted pumpkin seeds, and crumbled feta cheese, if desired.

7. Serve immediately or at room temperature.

NUTRITIONAL INFORMATION (PER SERVING, APPROXIMATE): Calories: 400, Fat: 15g, Saturated Fat: 2g, Cholesterol: 0mg, Sodium: 350mg, Carbohydrates: 50g, Fiber: 10g, Sugar: 10g, Protein: 15g

FATTOUSH SALAD WITH CRISPY PITA BREAD & HERBS

Prep Time: 15 minutes **Cooking Time**: 15 minutes **Total Time**: 30 minutes **Servings**: 4-6

Ingredients:

FOR THE SALAD:

- 2 large romaine lettuce heads, chopped
- 1 cucumber, thinly sliced
- 1 small red onion, thinly sliced
- 1 tomato, diced
-
- 1/2 cup fresh parsley, chopped
- 1/4 cup fresh mint, chopped
- 1/4 cup fresh dill, chopped (optional)
- 2 pita breads, torn into bite-sized pieces

FOR THE DRESSING:

- 1/4 cup olive oil
- 2 tablespoons lemon juice
- 1 tablespoon garlic, minced
- 1/2 teaspoon sumac (optional)
- Salt and black pepper to taste

OPTIONAL GARNISHES:

- Radishes, thinly sliced
- Green olives, halved
- Feta cheese crumbles
- Za'atar spice blend

Method:

- Toast the pita bread: Preheat oven to 400°F (200°C). Spread the pita bread pieces on a baking sheet and drizzle with olive oil. Bake for 10-15 minutes, or until golden brown and crispy.
- Combine the salad ingredients: In a large bowl, combine the chopped romaine lettuce,

cucumber, red onion, tomato, parsley, mint, and dill (if using).

- Make the dressing: Whisk together olive oil, lemon juice, garlic, sumac (if using), salt, and pepper in a small bowl.

- Assemble and serve: Add the crispy pita bread pieces to the salad and drizzle with the dressing. Toss gently to combine.
- Garnish with radishes, olives, feta cheese crumbles, and za'atar, if desired.
- Serve immediately at room temperature.

NUTRITIONAL INFORMATION (PER SERVING, APPROXIMATE):

Calories: 350, Fat: 15g, Saturated Fat: 2g, Cholesterol: 0mg, Sodium: 300mg, Carbohydrates: 30g, Fiber: 5g, Sugar: 5g, Protein: 5g

Prep Time: 20 minutes (plus marinating time) **Cooking Time**: 15-20 minutes **Total Time**: 35-45 minutes (depending on marinating time) **Servings**: 4-6

Ingredients:

FOR THE SHRIMP SKEWERS:

- 1 pound large shrimp, peeled and deveined
- 1/4 cup olive oil
- 2 tablespoons lemon juice
- 1 tablespoon chopped fresh oregano
- 1 teaspoon garlic powder
- 1/2 teaspoon salt
- 1/4 teaspoon black pepper
- Wooden skewers

FOR THE TZATZIKI DIP:

- 1 cup plain Greek yogurt
- 1/2 cucumber, seeded and grated
- 1 clove garlic, minced
- 1 tablespoon fresh dill, chopped
- 1 tablespoon lemon juice
- Salt and black pepper to taste

OPTIONAL GARNISHES:

- Lemon wedges
- Chopped fresh parsley
- Kalamata olives

Method:

1. Marinate the Shrimp: In a bowl, combine olive oil, lemon juice, oregano, garlic powder, salt, and pepper. Add the shrimp and toss to coat evenly. Cover and refrigerate for at least 1 hour, or up to overnight for richer flavor.

2. Prepare the Tzatziki Dip: Grate the cucumber and squeeze out excess moisture. In a bowl, combine Greek yogurt, cucumber, garlic, dill, lemon juice, salt, and pepper. Mix well and refrigerate until serving.

3. Prepare the Grill: Preheat grill to medium-high heat.

4. Thread the Skewers: Thread the marinated shrimp onto skewers.

5. Grill the Skewers: Grill the shrimp skewers for 3-4 minutes per side, or until cooked through to your desired doneness.

6. Assemble and Serve: Serve the shrimp skewers with a dollop of tzatziki dip on a platter.

7. Garnish with lemon wedges, chopped parsley, and Kalamata olives, if desired.

NUTRITIONAL INFORMATION (PER SERVING, APPROXIMATE) :

Calories: 450, Fat: 20g, Saturated Fat: 5g, Cholesterol: 100mg, Sodium: 400mg,, Carbohydrates: 30g, Fiber: 5g,, Sugar: 5g, Protein: 40g

MEDITERRANEAN STUFFED PORTOBELLO MUSHROOMS WITH GOAT CHEESE & HERBS.

Prep Time: 15 minutes **Cooking Time:** 20-25 minutes **Total Time:** 35-40 minutes **Servings**: 4

Ingredients:

- 4 large portobello mushrooms
- 2 tablespoons olive oil
- 1/2 onion, finely chopped
- 2 cloves garlic, minced
- 1/2 cup sun-dried tomatoes, chopped
- 4 ounces goat cheese, crumbled
- 1/4 cup chopped fresh parsley
- 1/4 cup chopped fresh basil

- 1 tablespoon chopped fresh mint
- Pinch of dried thyme
- Salt and black pepper to taste
- Optional Garnishes:
- Balsamic glaze
- Chopped fresh chives
- Roasted pine nuts

Method:

1. Preheat oven to 400°F (200°C).
2. Prepare the mushrooms: Gently brush the dirt off the portobello mushrooms. Remove the stems and carefully scrape out the gills with a spoon. Drizzle the mushroom caps with olive oil and season with salt and pepper.
3. Sauté the filling: Heat the remaining olive oil in a pan over medium heat. Add the onion and cook until softened, about 5 minutes. Add the garlic and cook for an additional minute until fragrant.
4. Stir in the chopped sun-dried tomatoes and cook for another minute.
5. Remove from heat and let cool slightly.
6. Assemble the Portobellos: In a bowl, combine the goat cheese, parsley, basil, mint, thyme, and the cooled filling. Season with salt and pepper to taste.
7. Spoon the mixture into the portobello mushroom caps, filling them generously.

8. Bake: Place the stuffed mushrooms on a baking sheet and bake for 20-25 minutes, or until the goat cheese is golden brown and bubbly.

9. Serve: Transfer the stuffed mushrooms to plates and drizzle with balsamic glaze, if desired.

10. Garnish with chopped chives and roasted pine nuts, if using.

NUTRITIONAL INFORMATION (PER SERVING, APPROXIMATE) :

Calories: 350, Fat: 20g, Saturated Fat: 5g, Cholesterol: 5mg, Sodium: 300mg,, Carbohydrates: 25g, Fiber: 5g, Sugar: 5g, Protein: 15g

SPICY CHICKPEA & MANGO FRITTERS WITH MINT YOGURT DIP.

Prep Time: 15 minutes **Cooking Time**: 20-25 minutes **Total Time**: 35-40 minutes **Servings**: 4-6

Ingredients:

FOR THE FRITTERS:

- 1 cup dried chickpeas, rinsed and soaked overnight
- 1 ripe mango, peeled and diced
- 1/2 cup chopped red onion
- 1/4 cup chopped fresh cilantro
- 1/4 cup chopped fresh mint
- 2 tablespoons chickpea flour

- 1 teaspoon garam masala
- 1/2 teaspoon chili powder (adjust to your spice preference)
- 1/4 teaspoon ground cumin
- 1/4 teaspoon turmeric
- Pinch of salt and black pepper
- Vegetable oil for frying

FOR THE MINT YOGURT DIP:

- 1 cup plain Greek yogurt
- 1/4 cup chopped fresh mint
- 1 tablespoon lemon juice
- Pinch of salt and black pepper

- Optional Garnishes:
- Lime wedges
- Chopped fresh parsley
- Sriracha sauce

Method:

1. Drain and mash the chickpeas: Drain the soaked chickpeas and mash them coarsely with a fork or food processor.
2. Combine the fritter ingredients: In a large bowl, combine the mashed chickpeas, diced mango, red onion, cilantro, mint, chickpea flour, garam masala, chili powder, cumin, turmeric, salt, and pepper. Mix well to form a thick batter.

3. Prepare the dip: In a small bowl, whisk together Greek yogurt, mint, lemon juice, salt, and pepper. Set aside.

4. Heat the oil: Heat about 1/2 inch of vegetable oil in a large skillet or dutch oven over medium-high heat.

5. Fry the fritters: Using a spoon or your hands, form the batter into small patties. Carefully drop the patties into the hot oil and fry for 2-3 minutes per side, or until golden brown and crispy.

6. Drain and serve: Drain the fritters on paper towels. Serve immediately with the mint yogurt dip, lime wedges, chopped parsley, and sriracha sauce, if desired.

NUTRITIONAL INFORMATION (PER SERVING, APPROXIMATE):

Calories: 300, Fat: 15g, Saturated Fat: 2g, Cholesterol: 0mg, Sodium: 300mg, Carbohydrates: 30g, Fiber: 5g, Sugar: 15g, Protein: 10g

WATERMELON & FETA SKEWERS WITH BALSAMIC GLAZE

Prep Time: 10 minutes **Cooking Time**: 0 minutes **Total Time**: 10 minutes **Servings**: 4-6

Ingredients:

- 2 cups seedless watermelon, cut into 1-inch cubes
- 1 cup feta cheese, cubed
- 1/4 cup fresh mint leaves
- 1/4 cup balsamic vinegar
- 1 tablespoon honey
- Pinch of black pepper
- Wooden skewers
- Optional Garnishes:
- Chopped fresh basil
- Crushed pistachios
- Balsamic pearls

Method:

1. Assemble the skewers: Thread watermelon cubes, feta cheese cubes, and mint leaves onto skewers, alternating ingredients as desired.
2. Make the balsamic glaze: In a small saucepan, combine balsamic vinegar, honey, and black pepper. Bring to a simmer over medium heat and cook until slightly thickened, about 5 minutes.
3. Serve: Drizzle the watermelon and feta skewers with the balsamic glaze.
4. Garnish with chopped fresh basil, crushed pistachios, and balsamic pearls, if desired.
5. Serve immediately and enjoy the cool refreshing flavors.

NUTRITIONAL INFORMATION (PER SERVING, APPROXIMATE):

Calories: 200, Fat: 5g, Saturated Fat: 2g, Cholesterol: 10mg, Sodium: 200mg

Carbohydrates: 30g, Fiber: 2g, Sugar: 25g, Protein: 5g

LENTIL & WALNUT PATTIES WITH LEMON TAHINI SAUCE.

Prep Time: 15 minutes **Cooking Time**: 20-25 minutes **Total Time**: 35-40 minutes **Servings**: 4-6

Ingredients:

FOR THE PATTIES:

- 1 cup dry brown lentils, rinsed
- 1/2 cup walnuts, chopped
- 1/2 cup breadcrumbs
- 1/4 cup chopped red onion
- 1/4 cup chopped fresh parsley
- 2 cloves garlic, minced
- 1 tablespoon olive oil
- 1 teaspoon lemon juice
- 1/2 teaspoon cumin
- 1/4 teaspoon salt
- Black pepper to taste

FOR THE LEMON TAHINI SAUCE:

- 1/3 cup tahini
- 1/4 cup lemon juice
- 2 tablespoons water
- 1 clove garlic, minced
- 1 tablespoon olive oil
- Pinch of salt
- Black pepper to taste

OPTIONAL GARNISHES:

- Chopped fresh dill
- Chopped cherry tomatoes
- Avocado slices
- Hummus

Method:

1. Cook the lentils: In a pot, combine lentils with 2 cups water. Bring to a boil, reduce heat, cover, and simmer for 20-25 minutes, or until tender. Drain and set aside to cool slightly.

2. Combine the patty ingredients: In a large bowl, mash the cooled lentils with a fork. Add chopped walnuts, breadcrumbs, red onion, parsley, garlic, olive oil, lemon juice, cumin, salt, and pepper. Mix well to combine and form a thick batter.

3. Shape the patties: Form the batter into equal-sized patties, about 1/2-inch thick.

4. Cook the patties: Heat a tablespoon of olive oil in a pan over medium heat. Add the patties and cook for 3-4 minutes per side, or until golden brown and crispy.

5. Make the sauce: In a bowl, whisk together tahini, lemon juice, water, garlic, olive oil, salt, and pepper until smooth and creamy.

6. Assemble and serve: Place the lentil and walnut patties on a plate and drizzle with the lemon tahini sauce.

7. Garnish with chopped dill, cherry tomatoes, avocado slices, or hummus, if desired.

NUTRITIONAL INFORMATION (PER SERVING, APPROXIMATE):

Calories: 400, Fat: 15g, Saturated Fat: 2g, Cholesterol: 0mg, Sodium: 350mg, Carbohydrates: 35g, Fiber: 10g, Sugar: 5g, Protein: 15g

Prep Time: 10 minutes (plus marinating time) **Cooking Time**: 25-30 minutes **Total Time**: 35-40 minutes
Servings: 4-6

Ingredients:

- 2 red bell peppers, sliced
- 1 yellow bell pepper, sliced
- 1 jar marinated artichoke hearts, drained and chopped
- 2 cloves garlic, minced
- 2 tablespoons olive oil
- 1/2 teaspoon dried oregano
- Salt and black pepper to taste
- 1 baguette, sliced into 1/2-inch thick pieces
- 4 ounces goat cheese, at room temperature
- Fresh basil leaves, for garnish (optional)

Method:

1. Preheat oven to 400°F (200°C).
2. Marinate the vegetables: In a bowl, combine sliced peppers, artichokes, garlic, olive oil, oregano, salt, and pepper. Toss to coat and let marinate for at least 15 minutes, or up to 30 minutes for deeper flavor.
3. Roast the vegetables: Spread the marinated vegetables on a baking sheet and roast for 25-30 minutes, or until tender and slightly browned.
4. Toast the baguette slices: Meanwhile, arrange the baguette slices on a separate baking sheet and toast in the oven for 5-7 minutes, or until lightly golden brown.
5. Assemble and serve: Spread each baguette slice with a dollop of goat cheese. Top with the roasted vegetables and garnish with fresh basil leaves, if desired.

NUTRITIONAL INFORMATION (PER SERVING, APPROXIMATE) : Calories: 300, Fat: 15g, Saturated Fat: 5g, Cholesterol: 10mg, Sodium: 300mg, Carbohydrates: 30g, Fiber: 5g, Sugar: 5g, Protein: 10g

CRISPY HALLOUMI & FIG SALAD WITH HONEY & MINT

Prep Time: 15 minutes **Cooking Time**: 10-12 minutes **Total Time**: 25-27 minutes **Servings**: 4

Ingredients:

FOR THE SALAD:

- 1/2 pound halloumi cheese, sliced into 1/2-inch thick pieces
- 2 tablespoons olive oil
- 8 ripe figs, quartered

- 1/2 red onion, thinly sliced
- 1/4 cup chopped fresh mint
- 1/4 cup fresh parsley, chopped (optional)

FOR THE DRESSING:

- 2 tablespoons honey
- 2 tablespoons olive oil
- 1 tablespoon lemon juice

- 1 teaspoon Dijon mustard
- Pinch of salt and black pepper

OPTIONAL GARNISHES:

- Balsamic glaze drizzle
- Chopped walnuts or pecans

- Crumbled feta cheese

1. **Method:**
2. Heat the oil: Heat olive oil in a pan over medium-high heat.
3. Cook the halloumi: Pan-fry the halloumi slices until golden brown and crispy on both sides, about 4-5 minutes per side.
4. Assemble the salad: While the halloumi is cooking, combine figs, red onion, mint, and parsley (if using) in a large bowl.

5. Make the dressing: In a small bowl, whisk together honey, olive oil, lemon juice, Dijon mustard, salt, and pepper.

6. Dress and serve: Once the halloumi is cooked, transfer it to the bowl with the salad ingredients. Drizzle with the dressing and toss gently to combine.

7. Garnish with balsamic glaze drizzle, chopped nuts, or crumbled feta cheese, if desired.

8. Serve immediately and enjoy the sweet and savory contrast.

NUTRITIONAL INFORMATION (PER SERVING, APPROXIMATE):

Calories: 400, Fat: 20g, Saturated Fat: 5g, Cholesterol: 60mg, Sodium: 300mg, Carbohydrates: 40g, Fiber: 5g, Sugar: 20g, Protein: 15g

WHITE BEAN & TUNA SALAD BOATS WITH TOASTED PITA BREAD

Prep Time: 15 minutes **Cooking Time**: 10 minutes (for pita bread) **Total Time**: 25 minutes **Servings**: 4

Ingredients:

FOR THE SALAD:

- 1 15-ounce can white beans, drained and rinsed
- 1 12-ounce can tuna, drained and flaked
- 1/2 cucumber, chopped
- 1/4 cup chopped red onion
- 1/4 cup chopped fresh parsley
- 2 tablespoons olive oil
- 1 tablespoon lemon juice
- 1 teaspoon dried oregano
- 1/2 teaspoon salt
- 1/4 teaspoon black pepper

FOR THE PITA BREAD BOATS:

- 4 large pita breads
- 2 tablespoons olive oil
- Pinch of salt
- Optional Garnishes:
- Chopped fresh dill
- Kalamata olives, sliced
- Feta cheese crumbles
- Lemon wedges

Method:

1. Preheat oven to 400°F (200°C).
2. Prepare the salad: In a large bowl, combine white beans, tuna, cucumber, red onion, and parsley.
3. Make the dressing: In a small bowl, whisk together olive oil, lemon juice, oregano, salt, and pepper.
4. Dress the salad: Pour the dressing over the bean and tuna mixture and toss gently to combine.

5. Toast the pita bread: Brush each pita bread with olive oil and sprinkle with a pinch of salt. Slice each pita in half, forming pockets, and arrange them on a baking sheet. Toast in the oven for 8-10 minutes, or until golden brown and crispy.

6. Assemble and serve: Fill each toasted pita bread boat with the tuna and white bean salad.

7. Garnish with chopped dill, olives, feta cheese crumbles, and lemon wedges, if desired.

8. Set sail for flavor and enjoy your Mediterranean voyage in every bite!

NUTRITIONAL INFORMATION (PER SERVING, APPROXIMATE) :

Calories: 400, Fat: 15g, Saturated Fat: 2g, Cholesterol: 50mg, Sodium: 400mg, Carbohydrates: 30g, Fiber: 5g, Sugar: 5g, Protein: 30g

CHAPTER FIVE

SOUPS AND STEWS

51. TOMATO AND WHITE BEAN SOUP WITH SPINACH AND MINT.

52. MOROCCAN CHICKPEA AND CARROT STEW WITH RAS EL HANOUT:

53. GREEK LEMON CHICKEN SOUP (AVGOLEMONO):

54. LENTIL AND SAUSAGE SOUP WITH KALE AND ROSEMARY

55. FISH AND SHELLFISH STEW WITH SAFFRON AND FENNEL

56. WHITE BEAN AND KALE MINESTRONE WITH PESTO

57. TURKISH LENTIL SOUP WITH RED PEPPER AND LEMON

58. TUSCAN WHITE BEAN AND CANNELLINI SOUP WITH HERBS

59. SPANISH GARLICKY SHRIMP SOUP WITH TOASTED BREAD

60. ITALIAN WHITE BEAN AND MUSSEL SOUP WITH FARRO

TOMATO AND WHITE BEAN SOUP WITH SPINACH AND MINT

Prep Time: 10 minutes **Cooking Time**: 20 minutes **Total Time:** 30 minutes **Servings**: 4

Ingredients:

- 1 tablespoon olive oil
- 1 large onion, diced
- 2 cloves garlic, minced
- 1 (28-ounce) can crushed tomatoes
- 4 cups vegetable broth
- 1 (15-ounce) can cannellini beans, drained and rinsed
- 1 cup fresh spinach
- 1/4 cup chopped fresh mint
- 1 tablespoon lemon juice
- Salt and black pepper to taste
- Garnish (optional): Fresh basil leaves, crusty bread

Method:

1. Heat olive oil in a large pot over medium heat. Add onion and cook until softened, about 5 minutes.
2. Add garlic and cook for 1 minute more, until fragrant.
3. Stir in crushed tomatoes, vegetable broth, and cannellini beans. Bring to a boil, then reduce heat and simmer for 15 minutes.
4. Add spinach and mint and cook until wilted, about 1-2 minutes.
5. Stir in lemon juice, salt, and pepper to taste.
6. Serve hot, garnished with fresh basil leaves and crusty bread, if desired.

NUTRITIONAL INFORMATION (PER SERVING, APPROXIMATE) :

Calories: 250, Fat: 5g, Saturated Fat: 1g, Cholesterol: 0mg, Sodium: 350mg, Carbohydrates: 35g, Fiber: 5g, Sugar: 5g, Protein: 10g

MOROCCAN CHICKPEA AND CARROT STEW WITH RAS EL HANOUT,

Prep Time: 15 minutes **Cooking Time**: 1 hour **Total Time:** 1 hour 15 minutes **Servings:** 6

Ingredients:

- 2 tablespoons olive oil
- 1 large onion, diced
- 2 cloves garlic, minced
- 1 teaspoon ground cumin
- 1 teaspoon ginger powder
- 1/2 teaspoon turmeric
- 1/4 teaspoon cayenne pepper (optional)
- 1 tablespoon tomato paste
- 1 (15-ounce) can diced tomatoes

- 4 cups vegetable broth
- 1 (15-ounce) can chickpeas, drained and rinsed
- 3 large carrots, peeled and roughly chopped
- 1 teaspoon ras el hanout spice blend
- 1/2 cup chopped fresh cilantro
- 1/4 cup chopped fresh parsley
- Salt and black pepper to taste
- Garnish (optional): Couscous, toasted almonds, lemon wedges

Method:

1. Heat olive oil in a large pot over medium heat. Add onion and cook until softened, about 5 minutes.
2. Stir in garlic, cumin, ginger, turmeric, and cayenne pepper (if using). Cook for 1 minute more, until fragrant.
3. Add tomato paste and cook for another minute, scraping the bottom of the pot.
4. Pour in diced tomatoes, vegetable broth, chickpeas, and carrots. Bring to a boil, then reduce heat and simmer for 45 minutes, or until carrots are tender.
5. Stir in ras el hanout, cilantro, and parsley. Season with salt and pepper to taste.

NUTRITIONAL INFORMATION (PER SERVING, APPROXIMATE): Calories: 350, Fat: 5g, Saturated Fat: 1g, Cholesterol: 0mg, Sodium: 400mg, Carbohydrates: 50g, Fiber: 10g, Sugar: 10g, Protein: 15g

GREEK LEMON CHICKEN SOUP (AVGOLEMONO)

Prep Time: 10 minutes **Cook Time**: 40 minutes **Total Time**: 50 minutes **Servings**: 6

Ingredients:

FOR THE SOUP:

- 1 tablespoon olive oil
- 1 onion, chopped
- 2 carrots, chopped
- 2 celery stalks, chopped
- 1 bay leaf

- 8 cups chicken broth
- 1 pound boneless, skinless chicken breasts, chopped
- 1/2 cup rice
- Salt and black pepper to taste

FOR THE AVGOLEMONO SAUCE:

- 2 egg yolks
- 1/4 cup fresh lemon juice

- 1/4 cup chicken broth, warmed
- Pinch of salt

Method:

1. Make the Soup: Heat olive oil in a large pot over medium heat. Add onion, carrots, and celery, and cook until softened, about 5 minutes.
2. Add bay leaf, chicken broth, and chopped chicken. Bring to a boil, then reduce heat and simmer for 20 minutes, or until chicken is cooked through.
3. Remove chicken from the pot and shred with two forks. Reserve the broth.
4. Add rice to the broth and cook for 10-15 minutes, or until tender.
5. Make the Avgolemono Sauce: In a separate bowl, whisk together egg yolks, lemon juice, warmed chicken broth, and salt until frothy and well combined.
6. Temper the egg mixture: Slowly add a ladleful of hot broth to the egg mixture, whisking constantly. Repeat with another ladleful.

7. Slowly return the tempered egg mixture to the pot with the rice and broth, whisking continuously to avoid curdling. Do not let the soup come to a boil.

8. Add shredded chicken back to the pot and stir gently to combine.

9. Serve hot, garnished with fresh dill or chopped parsley, if desired.

NUTRITIONAL INFORMATION (PER SERVING, APPROXIMATE):

Calories: 300, Fat: 5g, Saturated Fat: 1g, Cholesterol: 100mg, Sodium: 400mg, Carbohydrates: 35g, Fiber: 2g, Sugar: 2g. Protein: 25g

LENTIL AND SAUSAGE SOUP WITH KALE AND ROSEMARY

Prep Time: 15 minutes **Cook Time**: 40 minutes **Total Time**: 55 minutes **Servings**: 6

Ingredients:

- 2 tablespoons olive oil
- 1 large onion, chopped
- 2 cloves garlic, minced
- 1/2 pound bulk Italian sausage, casings removed
- 1 cup brown lentils, rinsed
- 4 cups vegetable broth

- 4 cups chopped kale
- 1 sprig fresh rosemary
- 1 (28-ounce) can crushed tomatoes
- 1/2 cup red wine (optional)
- Salt and black pepper to taste
- Parmesan cheese, grated (optional)
- Crusty bread, for serving

Method:

1. Heat olive oil in a large pot over medium heat. Add onion and cook until softened, about 5 minutes.
2. Add garlic and cook for 1 minute more, until fragrant.
3. Crumble the sausage into the pot and cook, breaking it up with a spoon, until browned.
4. Stir in lentils, vegetable broth, kale, rosemary sprig, and crushed tomatoes. Bring to a boil, then reduce heat and simmer for 30 minutes, or until lentils are tender.
5. Add red wine, if using, and simmer for an additional 5 minutes.
6. Season with salt and pepper to taste. Remove the rosemary sprig before serving.
7. Ladle the soup into bowls and sprinkle with grated Parmesan cheese, if desired. Serve with crusty bread for dipping.

NUTRITIONAL INFORMATION (PER SERVING, APPROXIMATE) : Calories: 400Fat: 10g,

Saturated Fat: 2g, Cholesterol: 50mg, Sodium: 500mg, Carbohydrates: 40g, Fiber: 10g. Sugar: 5g,

Protein: 20g

FISH AND SHELLFISH STEW WITH SAFFRON AND FENNEL,

Prep Time: 20 minutes **Cook Time**: 30 minutes **Total Time**: 50 minutes **Servings**: 4

Ingredients:

- 2 tablespoons olive oil
- 1 large fennel bulb, thinly sliced
- 1 onion, chopped
- 2 cloves garlic, minced
- 1/2 teaspoon dried thyme
- Pinch of saffron threads
- 1 cup dry white wine (e.g., Sauvignon Blanc)
- 4 cups fish broth

- 1 pound white fish fillets (e.g., cod, halibut, sea bass), cut into bite-sized pieces
- 1/2 pound mussels, debearded and cleaned
- 1/2 pound shrimp, peeled and deveined
- Salt and black pepper to taste
- Chopped fresh parsley, for garnish
- Crusty bread, for serving

Method:

1. Heat olive oil in a large pot or Dutch oven over medium heat. Add fennel and cook until softened and lightly golden, about 5 minutes.
2. Add onion and garlic, cook until softened, about 5 minutes more.
3. Stir in thyme and saffron threads, cook for 1 minute until fragrant.
4. Pour in white wine and simmer for 2 minutes, scraping up any browned bits from the bottom of the pot.
5. Add fish broth and bring to a simmer.
6. Gently add fish fillets and mussels, cover, and cook for 5-7 minutes, or until fish is just cooked through and mussels have opened.
7. Stir in shrimp and cook for an additional 1-2 minutes, or until pink and opaque.
8. Season with salt and pepper to taste.
9. Garnish with chopped parsley and serve hot with crusty bread for dipping.

NUTRITIONAL INFORMATION (PER SERVING, APPROXIMATE):

Calories: 450, Fat: 15g, Saturated Fat: 2g, Cholesterol: 150mg, Sodium: 500mg, Carbohydrates: 15g, Fiber: 2g, Sugar: 2g, Protein: 40g

WHITE BEAN AND KALE MINESTRONE WITH PESTO

Prep Time: 15 minutes **Cooking Time**: 40 minutes **Total Time**: 55 minutes **Servings**: 6

Ingredients:

- 2 tablespoons olive oil
- 1 large onion, chopped
- 2 cloves garlic, minced
- 1 carrot, chopped
- 2 celery stalks, chopped
- 1 teaspoon dried oregano
- 1/2 teaspoon dried thyme
- 4 cups vegetable broth
- 1 (15-ounce) can cannellini beans, drained and rinsed
- 1 (15-ounce) can white beans, drained and rinsed
- 1 (28-ounce) can crushed tomatoes
- 5 cups chopped kale
- 1/2 cup pesto
- Parmesan cheese, grated (for serving)
- Crusty bread, for serving (optional)

Method:

1. Heat olive oil in a large pot or Dutch oven over medium heat. Add onion and cook until softened, about 5 minutes.
2. Add garlic, carrot, and celery, cook for 5 minutes more until softened.
3. Stir in oregano and thyme, cook for 1 minute until fragrant.
4. Pour in vegetable broth and bring to a simmer.
5. Add cannellini beans, white beans, and crushed tomatoes. Increase heat and bring to a boil, then reduce heat and simmer for 15 minutes.
6. Stir in kale and cook for 5-7 minutes, or until tender.
7. Remove pot from heat and stir in pesto until well combined.
8. Ladle the soup into bowls and top with a generous sprinkle of parmesan cheese. Serve with crusty bread for dipping, if desired.

NUTRITIONAL INFORMATION (PER SERVING, APPROXIMATE):

Calories: 350, Fat: 10g, Saturated Fat: 2g, Cholesterol: 0mg, Sodium: 400mg, Carbohydrates: 45g, Fiber: 10g, Sugar: 5g, Protein: 15g

TURKISH LENTIL SOUP WITH RED PEPPER AND LEMON,

Prep Time: 15 minutes **Cook Time**: 40 minutes **Total Time**: 55 minutes **Servings**: 6

Ingredients:

- 2 tablespoons olive oil
- 1 large onion, chopped
- 2 cloves garlic, minced
- 1 red bell pepper, diced
- 1 tablespoon tomato paste
- 1 teaspoon ground cumin
- 1/2 teaspoon smoked paprika (optional)

- 4 cups vegetable broth
- 1 cup red lentils, rinsed
- 1/2 cup chopped fresh parsley
- Juice of 1 lemon
- Salt and black pepper to taste
- Garnish (optional): Red pepper flakes, lemon wedges, crusty bread

Method:

1. Heat olive oil in a large pot or Dutch oven over medium heat. Add onion and cook until softened, about 5 minutes.
2. Add garlic and red pepper, cook for 5 minutes more, until softened.
3. Stir in tomato paste, cumin, and paprika (if using), cook for 1 minute until fragrant.
4. Pour in vegetable broth and bring to a boil.
5. Add lentils and reduce heat to simmer. Cook for 30-35 minutes, or until lentils are tender.
6. Stir in parsley and lemon juice. Season with salt and pepper to taste.
7. Ladle the soup into bowls and garnish with red pepper flakes, lemon wedges, and crusty bread, if desired.

NUTRITIONAL INFORMATION (PER SERVING, APPROXIMATE) : Calories: 250, Fat: 5g, Saturated Fat: 1g, Cholesterol: 0mg, Sodium: 350mg, Carbohydrates: 35g, Fiber: 8g, Sugar: 5g, Protein: 15g

TUSCAN WHITE BEAN AND CANNELLINI SOUP WITH HERBS

Prep Time: 10 minutes **Cooking Time**: 40 minutes **Total Time**: 50 minutes **Servings**: 6

Ingredients:

- 2 tablespoons olive oil
- 1 onion, chopped
- 2 cloves garlic, minced
- 2 celery stalks, chopped
- 2 carrots, chopped
- 4 slices pancetta, diced
- 1/2 cup dry white wine (e.g., Pinot Grigio)
- 4 cups vegetable broth
- 1 (15-ounce) can cannellini beans, drained and rinsed
- 1 (15-ounce) can Great Northern beans, drained and rinsed
- 1 sprig fresh rosemary
- 1 sprig fresh thyme
- 1/2 teaspoon dried oregano
- 1/4 cup chopped fresh parsley
- Salt and black pepper to taste
- Garnish (optional): Extra virgin olive oil, crusty bread

Method:

1. Heat olive oil in a large pot or Dutch oven over medium heat. Add onion and cook until softened, about 5 minutes.
2. Add garlic, celery, and carrots, cook for 5 minutes more, until softened.
3. Add pancetta and cook until browned and crispy.
4. Pour in white wine and simmer for 2 minutes, scraping up any browned bits from the bottom of the pot.
5. Add vegetable broth, cannellini beans, Great Northern beans, rosemary, thyme, and oregano. Bring to a boil, then reduce heat and simmer for 20 minutes.
6. Remove the herb sprigs and discard.
7. Stir in parsley and season with salt and pepper to taste.

8. Ladle the soup into bowls and drizzle with a touch of extra virgin olive oil, if desired. Serve with crusty bread for dipping.

NUTRITIONAL INFORMATION (PER SERVING, APPROXIMATE) :

Calories: 300, Fat: 10g, Saturated Fat: 2g, Cholesterol: 10mg, Sodium: 400mg, Carbohydrates: 40g, Fiber: 8g, Sugar: 5g, Protein: 15g

SPANISH GARLICKY SHRIMP SOUP WITH TOASTED BREAD

Prep Time: 15 minutes **Cooking Time**: 20 minutes **Total Time**: 35 minutes **Servings**: 4

Ingredients:

FOR THE SOUP:

- 1/4 cup olive oil
- 6 cloves garlic, thinly sliced
- 1/2 teaspoon smoked paprika
- 1 pinch red pepper flakes (optional)
- 1/2 cup dry white wine (e.g., Sauvignon Blanc)
- 4 cups fish broth
- 1 pound large shrimp, peeled and deveined
- 1/4 cup chopped fresh parsley
- Salt and black pepper to taste

FOR THE TOASTED BREAD:

- 4 slices crusty bread (e.g., baguette, ciabatta)
- 1 tablespoon olive oil
- 1 clove garlic, halved

Method:

1. Make the Soup: Heat olive oil in a large pot or Dutch oven over medium heat. Add garlic and cook until golden brown and fragrant, about 5 minutes. Do not burn the garlic.
2. Stir in paprika and red pepper flakes (if using), cook for 30 seconds.
3. Pour in white wine and simmer for 2 minutes, scraping up any browned bits from the bottom of the pot.
4. Add fish broth and bring to a boil. Reduce heat and simmer for 5 minutes.
5. Add shrimp and cook for 3-4 minutes, or until pink and opaque. Do not overcook.
6. Stir in parsley and season with salt and pepper to taste.
7. Toast the Bread: While the soup simmers, rub the halved garlic clove on both sides of the bread slices.

8. Heat olive oil in a separate pan over medium heat. Toast the bread on both sides until golden brown and crispy.

NUTRITIONAL INFORMATION (PER SERVING, APPROXIMATE): Calories: 350, Fat: 15g, Saturated Fat: 2g, Cholesterol: 200mg, Sodium: 400mg, Carbohydrates: 25g, Fiber: 2g, Sugar: 2g, Protein: 30g

ITALIAN WHITE BEAN AND MUSSEL SOUP WITH FARRO

Prep Time: 15 minutes **Cooking Time**: 40 minutes **Total Time**: 55 minutes **Servings**: 6

Ingredients:

- 2 tablespoons olive oil
- 1 large onion, chopped
- 2 cloves garlic, minced
- 1 celery stalk, chopped
- 1 carrot, chopped
- 1/2 teaspoon dried thyme
- 1/4 teaspoon red pepper flakes (optional)
- 1 (28-ounce) can whole peeled tomatoes, crushed by hand

- 4 cups vegetable broth
- 1 cup dried white beans (e.g., cannellini, Great Northern)
- 1 pound mussels, debearded and cleaned
- 1/2 cup farro grains
- 1/4 cup chopped fresh parsley
- Salt and black pepper to taste
- Lemon wedges (optional)
- Crusty bread, for serving (optional)

Method:

1. Heat olive oil in a large pot or Dutch oven over medium heat. Add onion and cook until softened, about 5 minutes.
2. Add garlic, celery, and carrot, cook for 5 minutes more, until softened.
3. Stir in thyme and red pepper flakes (if using), cook for 1 minute until fragrant.
4. Add crushed tomatoes and vegetable broth. Bring to a boil, then reduce heat and simmer for 15 minutes.
5. Add white beans and simmer for 20 minutes, or until beans are tender.
6. Add mussels and farro, cover, and cook for 5-7 minutes, or until mussels have opened and farro is tender. Discard any unopened mussels.
7. Stir in parsley and season with salt and pepper to taste.
8. Ladle the soup into bowls and serve with lemon wedges and crusty bread, if desired.

NUTRITIONAL INFORMATION (PER SERVING, APPROXIMATE) :

Calories: 400, Fat: 10g, Saturated Fat: 2g, Cholesterol: 50mg, Sodium: 450mg, Carbohydrates: 50g, Fiber: 10g, Sugar: 5g, Protein: 25g

CHAPTER SIX

WHOLESOME MAIN COURSES

61. LEMON & THYME ROASTED CHICKEN WITH CHICKPEAS & ARTICHOKES

62. CRISPY BAKED COD WITH RATATOUILLE:

63. SPICED CHICKPEA & SWEET POTATO SHEPHERD'S PIE

64. CREAMY MASHED SWEET POTATOES AND BAKED UNTIL GOLDEN BROWN.

65. BAKED STUFFED PEPPERS WITH QUINOA & SPINACH

66. GREEK MOUSSAKA WITH ZUCCHINI NOODLES

67. SHRIMP SAGANAKI WITH FETA & SPINACH

68. BAKED FALAFEL BOWLS WITH TAHINI SAUCE & ROASTED VEGETABLES

69. HERB-CRUSTED LAMB MEATBALLS WITH YOGURT SAUC.

70. ROASTED CAULIFLOWER STEAK WITH ROMESCO SAUCE & MARINATED ARTICHOKES

LEMON & THYME ROASTED CHICKEN WITH CHICKPEAS & ARTICHOKES

Prep Time: 15 minutes **Cooking Time**: 1 hour 20 minutes **Total Time:** 1 hour 35 minutes **Servings:** 4-6 (depending on chicken size)

Ingredients:

FOR THE CHICKEN:

- 1 whole fryer chicken (3-4 pounds)
- 1 tablespoon olive oil
- 1 teaspoon dried thyme

- 1/2 teaspoon smoked paprika
- 1/2 teaspoon garlic powder
- Salt and black pepper to taste

FOR THE ROASTED VEGETABLES:

- 1 (15-ounce) can chickpeas, drained and rinsed
- 1 (14-ounce) can artichoke hearts, quartered
- 1/2 cup halved sun-dried tomatoes
- 1 red onion, chopped

- 2 cloves garlic, minced
- 1/4 cup white wine (optional)
- 1/4 cup chicken broth
- Juice of 1 lemon
- 1/4 cup chopped fresh parsley (optional)

Method:

1. Preheat oven to 425°F (220°C).
2. Prep the Chicken: Pat the chicken dry and truss it if desired. Drizzle with olive oil and rub with thyme, paprika, garlic powder, salt, and pepper.
3. Roast the Chicken: Place the chicken breast-side up in a large oven-safe dish. Scatter the chickpeas, artichokes, sun-dried tomatoes, onion, and garlic around the chicken.

4. Deglaze and Simmer: If using white wine, pour it into the bottom of the pan. Scrape up any browned bits and bring to a simmer on the stovetop for 1 minute. Pour in the chicken broth and lemon juice.

5. Bake and Baste: Return the dish to the oven and roast for 1 hour, or until the chicken is cooked through and juices run clear when pierced with a knife. Baste the chicken with the pan juices every 15-20 minutes.

6. Finish and Garnish: Transfer the chicken to a cutting board and let rest for 10 minutes before carving. Stir the parsley into the roasted vegetables, if using.

7. Serve: Arrange the roasted vegetables and chicken on a platter and drizzle with pan juices.

NUTRITIONAL INFORMATION (PER SERVING, APPROXIMATE):

Calories: 500, Fat: 25g, Saturated Fat: 5g, Cholesterol: 150mg, Sodium: 500mg, Carbohydrates: 40g, Fiber: 10g, Sugar: 5g, Protein: 45g

CRISPY BAKED COD WITH RATATOUILLE

Prep Time: 15 minutes **Cooking Time**: 40 minutes **Total Time:** 55 minutes **Servings**: 4

Ingredients:

FOR THE RATATOUILLE:

- 2 tablespoons olive oil
- 1 medium onion, chopped
- 1 red bell pepper, chopped
- 1 yellow bell pepper, chopped
- 1 zucchini, chopped
- 1 eggplant, chopped

- 2 cloves garlic, minced
- 1 (14.5-ounce) can diced tomatoes, undrained
- 1/2 teaspoon dried oregano
- 1/4 teaspoon dried thyme
- Salt and black pepper to taste

FOR THE COD:

- 4 cod fillets (around 6 ounces each)
- 1/4 cup all-purpose flour
- 1/4 teaspoon paprika

- 1/8 teaspoon garlic powder
- Salt and black pepper to taste
- 2 tablespoons olive oil

Method:

1. Preheat oven to 400°F (200°C).
2. Prep the Ratatouille: Heat olive oil in a large oven-proof skillet or Dutch oven over medium heat. Add onion and cook until softened, about 5 minutes.
3. Add bell peppers, zucchini, and eggplant, cook for 5 minutes more, until softened.
4. Stir in garlic, diced tomatoes, oregano, thyme, salt, and pepper. Bring to a simmer and cook for 10 minutes, stirring occasionally.

5. Prep the Cod: While the ratatouille simmers, pat the cod fillets dry with paper towels. Season with salt and pepper.

6. In a shallow dish, combine flour, paprika, and garlic powder. Dredge each cod fillet in the flour mixture, coating both sides.

7. Bake the Cod: Heat olive oil in a separate oven-proof pan over medium-high heat. Sear the cod fillets for 2-3 minutes per side, until golden brown and crispy.

8. Finish and Serve: Transfer the cod fillets to the simmering ratatouille and arrange them on top. Bake in the preheated oven for 10-12 minutes, or until the cod is cooked through and flakes easily.

NUTRITIONAL INFORMATION (PER SERVING, APPROXIMATE) :

Calories: 400, Fat: 15g, Saturated Fat: 2g, Cholesterol: 80mg, Sodium: 400mg, Carbohydrates: 30g, Fiber: 5g, Sugar: 5g, Protein: 40g

CRISPY BAKED COD WITH RATATOUILLE: A LIGHT & FLAVORFUL FEAST

Prep Time: 15 minutes **Cooking Time**: 40 minutes **Total Time**: 55 minutes **Servings**: 4

Ingredients:

FOR THE RATATOUILLE:

- 2 tablespoons olive oil
- 1 medium onion, chopped
- 1 red bell pepper, chopped
- 1 yellow bell pepper, chopped
- 1 zucchini, chopped
- 1 eggplant, chopped

- 2 cloves garlic, minced
- 1 (14.5-ounce) can diced tomatoes, undrained
- 1/2 teaspoon dried oregano
- 1/4 teaspoon dried thyme
- Salt and black pepper to taste

FOR THE COD:

- 4 cod fillets (around 6 ounces each)
- 1/4 cup all-purpose flour
- 1/4 teaspoon paprika

- 1/8 teaspoon garlic powder
- Salt and black pepper to taste
- 2 tablespoons olive oil

Method:

1. Preheat oven to 400°F (200°C).
2. Prep the Ratatouille: Heat olive oil in a large oven-proof skillet or Dutch oven over medium heat. Add onion and cook until softened, about 5 minutes.
3. Add bell peppers, zucchini, and eggplant, cook for 5 minutes more, until softened.
4. Stir in garlic, diced tomatoes, oregano, thyme, salt, and pepper. Bring to a simmer and cook for 10 minutes, stirring occasionally.

5. Prep the Cod: While the ratatouille simmers, pat the cod fillets dry with paper towels. Season with salt and pepper.

6. In a shallow dish, combine flour, paprika, and garlic powder. Dredge each cod fillet in the flour mixture, coating both sides.

7. Bake the Cod: Heat olive oil in a separate oven-proof pan over medium-high heat. Sear the cod fillets for 2-3 minutes per side, until golden brown and crispy.

8. Finish and Serve: Transfer the cod fillets to the simmering ratatouille and arrange them on top. Bake in the preheated oven for 10-12 minutes, or until the cod is cooked through and flakes easily.

NUTRITIONAL INFORMATION (PER SERVING, APPROXIMATE):

Calories: 400, Fat: 15g, Saturated Fat: 2g, Cholesterol: 80mg, Sodium: 400mg, Carbohydrates: 30g, Fiber: 5g, Sugar: 5g, Protein: 40g

CREAMY MASHED SWEET POTATOES AND BAKED UNTIL GOLDEN BROWN.

Prep Time: 15 minutes **Cooking Time:** 45-50 minutes **Total Time:** 60 minutes **Servings**: 4-6 (depending on appetites)

Ingredients:

- 2 large sweet potatoes (around 1 pound each)
- 1 tablespoon olive oil
- 1/2 teaspoon sea salt
- Black pepper to taste
- 1/4 cup butter, softened
- 1/4 cup milk (can adjust for desired consistency)
- 1/4 teaspoon ground cinnamon (optional)
- 1/4 teaspoon freshly grated nutmeg (optional)
- Pinch of cloves (optional)

Method:

1. Preheat oven to 400°F (200°C).
2. Prep the Sweet Potatoes: Wash and dry the sweet potatoes. Poke them all over with a fork.
3. Roast the Sweet Potatoes: Rub each potato with olive oil and sprinkle with salt. Place them on a baking sheet and bake for 45-50 minutes, or until tender when pierced with a fork.
4. Scoop and Mash: Let the potatoes cool slightly, then cut them open and scoop out the flesh into a large bowl. Discard the skins.
5. Cream the Mash: Using a potato masher or hand mixer, cream the sweet potatoes until smooth and fluffy. Gradually add the softened butter, milk, and spices (if using), adjusting the milk for desired consistency. Season with black pepper to taste.
6. Spread and Bake: Transfer the mashed sweet potatoes to an oven-proof baking dish. Smooth the top and create peaks with a fork for texture.

7. Brown and Glaze: Bake the mashed sweet potatoes for 10-15 minutes, or until the top is golden brown and bubbly. You can also broil for a few minutes to achieve a deeper caramelization, watching closely to avoid burning.

NUTRITIONAL INFORMATION (PER SERVING, APPROXIMATE) :

Calories: 250, Fat: 8g, Saturated Fat: 4g, Cholesterol: 20mg, Sodium: 130mg, Carbohydrates: 40g, Fiber: 5g, Sugar: 10g, Protein: 2g

Prep Time: 15 minutes **Cooking Time**: 45 minutes **Total Time**: 60 minutes **Servings**: 4-6 (depending on pepper size)

Ingredients:

FOR THE PEPPERS:

- 4 large bell peppers (red, yellow, orange, or a mix)
- For the Quinoa Stuffing:
- 1 cup quinoa, rinsed
- 1 1/2 cups vegetable broth
- 1 tablespoon olive oil
- 1/2 onion, chopped
- 2 cloves garlic, minced
- 1/2 cup chopped cherry tomatoes
- 1/4 cup cooked black beans, rinsed and drained (optional)
- 1/4 cup chopped fresh parsley
- 1/4 cup chopped fresh spinach
- 1/2 teaspoon cumin
- 1/4 teaspoon smoked paprika
- 1/4 teaspoon chili powder (optional)
- Salt and black pepper to taste

FOR THE TOPPING (OPTIONAL):

- 1/4 cup crumbled feta cheese
- Fresh herbs, such as basil or cilantro

Method:

1. Preheat oven to 400°F (200°C).
2. Prep the Peppers: Wash and dry the bell peppers. Cut off the tops and remove the seeds and membranes. Place the pepper "cups" upright on a baking sheet.
3. Cook the Quinoa: In a saucepan, combine rinsed quinoa and vegetable broth. Bring to a boil, then reduce heat, cover, and simmer for 15 minutes, or until fluffy and cooked through.

4. Sauté the Vegetables: While the quinoa cooks, heat olive oil in a large skillet over medium heat. Add onion and cook until softened, about 5 minutes.

5. Add garlic and cook for 30 seconds until fragrant. Stir in cherry tomatoes, black beans (if using), parsley, and spinach. Cook for 3-4 minutes, until spinach wilts.

6. Season and Combine: Transfer the cooked quinoa to the skillet with the vegetables. Stir in cumin, paprika, chili powder (if using), salt, and pepper. Mix well to combine.

7. Stuff and Bake: Fill the prepared pepper cups with the quinoa mixture, packing it loosely. Arrange them on the baking sheet and bake for 30-35 minutes, or until the peppers are tender and the filling is heated through.

8. Optional Topping: Sprinkle crumbled feta cheese and fresh herbs over the baked peppers before serving.

NUTRITIONAL INFORMATION (PER SERVING, APPROXIMATE):

Calories: 350, Fat: 5g, Saturated Fat: 1g, Cholesterol: 0mg, Sodium: 350mg, Carbohydrates: 50g, Fiber: 8g, Sugar: 5g, Protein: 15g

Prep Time: 20 minutes **Cooking Time**: 55 minutes **Total Time:** 75 minutes **Servings:** 4-6

Ingredients:

FOR THE ZUCCHINI NOODLES:

- 2 large zucchinis
- 1 tablespoon olive oil
- Salt and black pepper to taste
- For the Meat Sauce:
- 1 tablespoon olive oil
- 1 onion, chopped
- 2 cloves garlic, minced

- 1 pound ground lamb or beef (can use vegetarian crumbles for a meatless option)
- 1/2 teaspoon dried oregano
- 1/4 teaspoon ground cinnamon
- 1 (14.5-ounce) can diced tomatoes, undrained
- 1/2 cup red wine (optional)
- Salt and black pepper to taste

FOR THE BéCHAMEL SAUCE:

- 3 tablespoons butter
- 3 tablespoons all-purpose flour
- 3 cups milk, warmed

- 1/2 teaspoon grated nutmeg
- Salt and black pepper to taste

FOR THE TOPPING:

- 1/2 cup grated Parmesan cheese
- 1/4 cup chopped fresh parsley

Method:

1. Prep the Zucchini: Using a spiralizer, create noodles from the zucchini. Season with olive oil, salt, and pepper, and set aside.

2. Brown the Meat: Heat olive oil in a large skillet over medium heat. Add onion and cook until softened, about 5 minutes.

3. Add garlic and cook for 30 seconds until fragrant. Stir in the ground meat and cook, breaking it up with a spoon, until browned.

4. Add Seasonings and Simmer: Sprinkle in oregano and cinnamon. Add the diced tomatoes and red wine (if using). Bring to a simmer and cook for 15 minutes, stirring occasionally. Season with salt and pepper to taste.

5. Make the Béchamel: In a separate saucepan, melt butter over medium heat. Whisk in flour and cook for 1 minute. Gradually whisk in the warmed milk until smooth and thick. Add nutmeg, salt, and pepper to taste.

6. Assemble and Bake: Preheat oven to 375°F (190°C). Spread a thin layer of meat sauce in an oven-proof dish. Arrange half of the zucchini noodles on top. Repeat with another layer of meat sauce and the remaining zucchini noodles. Pour the béchamel sauce over the top, spreading evenly.

7. Bake and Brown: Sprinkle with Parmesan cheese. Bake for 30-35 minutes, or until the top is golden brown and bubbly.

8. Garnish and Serve: Let the moussaka rest for 10 minutes before serving. Garnish with chopped parsley and enjoy a lighter, veggie-packed take on a Greek classic!

NUTRITIONAL INFORMATION (PER SERVING, APPROXIMATE) :

Calories: 400, Fat: 15g, Saturated Fat: 5g, Cholesterol: 60mg, Sodium: 500mg, Carbohydrates: 35g, Fiber: 5g, Sugar: 5g, Protein: 30g

Prep Time: 15 minutes **Cooking Time**: 20 minutes **Total Time**: 35 minutes **Servings**: 4

Ingredients:

FOR THE SAGANAKI:

- 1/4 cup extra virgin olive oil
- 6 cloves garlic, thinly sliced
- 1/2 teaspoon smoked paprika
- Pinch of red pepper flakes (optional)
- 1/2 cup dry white wine (e.g., Sauvignon Blanc)
- 4 cups fish broth
- 1 pound large shrimp, peeled and deveined
- 1/4 cup chopped fresh parsley
- Salt and black pepper to taste

FOR THE SPINACH:

- 1 tablespoon olive oil
- 1/2 onion, chopped
- 2 cloves garlic, minced
- 8 ounces fresh spinach, washed and stemmed
- 1/4 cup crumbled feta cheese

Method:

1. Sizzle the Garlic: Heat olive oil in a large skillet or Dutch oven over medium heat. Add the sliced garlic and cook, stirring occasionally, until golden brown and fragrant, about 5 minutes. Watch closely to avoid burning the garlic, as it can turn bitter.

2. Infuse the Paprika: Stir in the paprika and red pepper flakes (if using) and cook for 30 seconds, allowing the smoky aroma to bloom.

3. Deglaze and Simmer: Pour in the white wine and simmer for 2 minutes, scraping up any browned bits from the bottom of the pan. This deglazing step adds depth and flavor to the broth.

4. Build the Broth: Add the fish broth and bring to a boil. Reduce heat and simmer for 5 minutes, allowing the flavors to meld.

5. Plump the Shrimp: Dive in the shrimp and cook for 3-4 minutes, or until pink and opaque. Watch carefully to avoid overcooking, as they will become tough.

6. Spinach Symphony: In a separate pan, heat olive oil over medium heat. Add onion and cook until softened, about 5 minutes. Stir in garlic and cook for 30 seconds until fragrant. Add the spinach and cook until wilted, about 1 minute.

7. Finishing Touches: Stir the cooked spinach into the shrimp and broth. Add crumbled feta cheese and season with salt and pepper to taste. Let the soup rest for a minute before serving to allow the flavors to further harmonize.

NUTRITIONAL INFORMATION (PER SERVING, APPROXIMATE):

Calories: 350, Fat: 15g, Saturated Fat: 2g, Cholesterol: 200mg, Sodium: 400mg,, Carbohydrates: 25g

Fiber: 2g, Sugar: 2g, Protein: 30g

BAKED FALAFEL BOWLS WITH TAHINI SAUCE & ROASTED VEGETABLES

Prep Time: 15 minutes **Cook Time**: 40 minutes **Total Time**: 55 minutes **Servings**: 4

Ingredients:

FOR THE FALAFEL:

- 1 (15-ounce) can dried chickpeas, soaked overnight or for at least 8 hours (optional)
- 1/2 cup chopped onion
- 1/2 cup chopped parsley
- 1/4 cup chopped cilantro
- 3 cloves garlic, minced
- 1/2 teaspoon cumin
- 1/4 teaspoon coriander
- 1/4 teaspoon paprika
- Salt and black pepper to taste
- 1/4 cup breadcrumbs (optional)
- For the Roasted Vegetables:
- 1 red bell pepper, chopped
- 1 yellow bell pepper, chopped
- 1 zucchini, chopped
- 1/2 red onion, chopped
- 1 tablespoon olive oil
- Salt and black pepper to taste

FOR THE TAHINI SAUCE:

- 1/4 cup tahini
- 2 tablespoons lemon juice
- 2 tablespoons water
- 1 clove garlic, minced
- 2 tablespoons olive oil

FOR THE BOWLS:

- 4 cups cooked quinoa or brown rice (optional)
- 1/2 cup chopped cucumber
- 1/4 cup chopped cherry tomatoes

- 1/4 cup crumbled feta cheese (optional)
- Fresh herbs, such as parsley and cilantro, for garnish

Method:

1. Prep the Falafel: Drain and rinse the soaked chickpeas, if using. Combine them in a food processor with onion, parsley, cilantro, garlic, cumin, coriander, paprika, salt, and pepper. Pulse until coarsely chopped, stopping to scrape down the sides as needed. Add breadcrumbs, if using, and pulse a few more times to combine.

2. Form the Falafel: Shape the falafel mixture into balls about the size of ping pong balls. Place them on a baking sheet lined with parchment paper.

3. Bake the Falafel: Preheat oven to 400°F (200°C). Bake the falafel for 20-25 minutes, or until golden brown and firm. Flip them halfway through baking for even browning.

4. Roast the Vegetables: While the falafel bakes, toss the bell peppers, zucchini, and red onion with olive oil, salt, and pepper. Spread them on a separate baking sheet and roast for 15-20 minutes, or until tender and slightly browned.

5. Make the Tahini Sauce: In a small bowl, whisk together tahini, lemon juice, water, garlic, olive oil, salt, and pepper. Adjust the consistency with additional water if needed.

6. Assemble the Bowls: Divide the cooked quinoa or brown rice (if using) into bowls. Top with falafel, roasted vegetables, chopped cucumber and tomatoes, crumbled feta cheese (if using), and a generous drizzle of tahini sauce. Garnish with fresh herbs and savor the explosion of flavors!

NUTRITIONAL INFORMATION (PER SERVING, APPROXIMATE) :

Calories: 500, Fat: 15g, Saturated Fat: 2g, Cholesterol: 0mg, Sodium: 400mg, Carbohydrates: 60g, Fiber: 10g, Sugar: 5g, Protein: 20g

HERB-CRUSTED LAMB MEATBALLS WITH YOGURT SAUC.

Prep Time: 15 minutes **Cooking Time**: 25 minutes **Total Time**: 40 minutes **Servings**: 4-6

Ingredients:

FOR THE LAMB MEATBALLS:

- 1 pound ground lamb
- 1/2 cup finely chopped fresh herbs (mix and match like parsley, mint, oregano, thyme)
- 1/4 cup breadcrumbs
- 1/2 teaspoon grated onion
- 1/2 teaspoon garlic powder
- 1/4 teaspoon cumin
- Salt and black pepper to taste

- Olive oil for drizzling
- For the Yogurt Sauce:
- 1 cup plain Greek yogurt
- 1/4 cup finely chopped fresh dill
- 1 tablespoon lemon juice
- 1 clove garlic, minced
- Salt and black pepper to taste

OPTIONAL GARNISHES:

- Chopped fresh herbs
- Crumbled feta cheese

- Sliced red onion
- Lemon wedges

Method:

1. Preheat oven to 400°F (200°C). Line a baking sheet with parchment paper.
2. Combine the lamb meatball ingredients: In a large bowl, mix together the ground lamb, chopped herbs, breadcrumbs, grated onion, garlic powder, cumin, salt, and pepper.
3. Form the meatballs: Roll the mixture into bite-sized balls, about 1-1.5 inches in diameter. Drizzle them with olive oil.

4. Bake the meatballs: Arrange the meatballs on the prepared baking sheet and bake for 20-25 minutes, or until cooked through and golden brown.

5. Make the yogurt sauce: While the meatballs bake, whisk together the Greek yogurt, dill, lemon juice, garlic, salt, and pepper in a small bowl. Adjust the seasonings to your taste.

6. Assemble and serve: Arrange the cooked meatballs on a platter or in individual bowls. Spoon the yogurt sauce over them and garnish with your chosen toppings. Enjoy the burst of flavor and freshness in every bite!

NUTRITIONAL INFORMATION (PER SERVING, APPROXIMATE) :, Calories: 350, Fat: 20g, Saturated Fat: 8g, Cholesterol: 70mg, Sodium: 300mg, Carbohydrates: 10g, Fiber: 1g, Sugar: 2g, Protein: 30g

ROASTED CAULIFLOWER STEAK WITH ROMESCO SAUCE & MARINATED ARTICHOKES

Prep Time: 15 minutes **Cooking Time**: 45 minutes **Total Time**: 60 minutes **Servings**: 2-3

Ingredients:

FOR THE CAULIFLOWER STEAKS:

- 1 large head cauliflower
- 1 tablespoon olive oil
- Salt and black pepper to taste
- For the Romesco Sauce:
- 1 red bell pepper, roasted and peeled (can use jarred roasted peppers)
- 2 roasted tomatoes (can use canned fire-roasted tomatoes)
- 1/4 cup almonds, toasted (or walnuts, cashews, pecans)
- 2 cloves garlic
- 1 tablespoon smoked paprika
- 1/2 teaspoon sherry vinegar (or red wine vinegar)
- 1/4 cup olive oil
- Salt and black pepper to taste

FOR THE MARINATED ARTICHOKES:

- 1 jar marinated artichoke hearts, drained and quartered
- For Serving (optional):
- Chopped fresh parsley
- Crumbled feta cheese
- Microgreens

Method:

1. Preheat oven to 400°F (200°C). Line a baking sheet with parchment paper.

2. Prep the Cauliflower Steaks: Cut the cauliflower head into 1-inch thick slices, creating "steaks." Trim the bottoms to ensure they sit flat. Brush each steak with olive oil and season generously with salt and pepper. Arrange them on the prepared baking sheet.

3. Roast the Cauliflower Steaks: Bake for 30-35 minutes, or until tender and slightly golden brown. Flip them halfway through baking for even cooking.

4. Make the Romesco Sauce: While the cauliflower cooks, blend the roasted red pepper, tomatoes, almonds, garlic, paprika, vinegar, and olive oil in a food processor until smooth. Season with salt and pepper to taste. You can adjust the consistency by adding a little water if needed.

5. Assemble and Serve: Spread a generous layer of romesco sauce on each cauliflower steak. Top with artichoke hearts and garnish with chopped parsley, crumbled feta cheese, and microgreens (if using). Enjoy the symphony of flavors in every bite!

NUTRITIONAL INFORMATION (PER SERVING, APPROXIMATE):

Calories: 450, Fat: 20g, Saturated Fat: 3g, Cholesterol: 0mg, Sodium: 300mg, Carbohydrates: 50g, Fiber: 8g, Sugar: 10g, Protein: 15g

CHAPTER SEVEN

VIBRANT SIDES AND ACCOMPANIMENTS

71. **ROASTED GREEK LEMON POTATOES**

72. **LEMONY QUINOA SALAD WITH HERBS & TOMATOES**

73. **GRILLED HALLOUMI & WATERMELON SALAD**

74. **SPICED CHICKPEA FRITTERS WITH TAHINI SAUCE**

75. **ROASTED GREEK FETA DIP WITH PITA BREAD**

76. **GREEK YOGURT TZATZIKI SAUCE**

77. **GARLIC & HERB CRUSTED ZUCCHINI FRIES**

78. **MARINATED ARTICHOKE HEARTS WITH OLIVES & HERBS**

79. **ROASTED BRUSSELS SPROUTS WITH BALSAMIC GLAZE & GOAT CHEESE**

80. **GREEK LEMON RICE PILAF**

Prep Time: 15 minutes **Cooking Time**: 45-50 minutes **Total Time**: 60 minutes **Servings**: 4-6

Ingredients:

- 2 pounds potatoes (choose Yukon Gold or russet)
- 1/4 cup olive oil
- 2 tablespoons lemon juice
- 2 cloves garlic, minced

- 1 teaspoon dried oregano
- 1/2 teaspoon salt
- 1/4 teaspoon black pepper
- Fresh parsley, chopped (optional, for garnish)

Method:

1. Preheat oven to 425°F (220°C). Line a baking sheet with parchment paper.
2. Prep the Potatoes: Wash and dry the potatoes. Cut them into 1-inch thick wedges, ensuring they are roughly equal in size for even cooking.
3. Make the Lemon Herb Coating: In a large bowl, whisk together olive oil, lemon juice, garlic, oregano, salt, and pepper.
4. Toss and Coat: Add the potato wedges to the lemony mixture and toss well to coat evenly. Ensure each piece is covered in the flavorful marinade.
5. Spread and Roast: Spread the seasoned potato wedges on the prepared baking sheet in a single layer, leaving space between them for optimal crisping.
6. Kiss them with Fire: Roast the potatoes for 45-50 minutes, flipping them halfway through cooking. They should be golden brown and fork-tender when done.
7. Optional Garnish: Sprinkle chopped fresh parsley over the roasted potatoes for a touch of color and freshness.
8. Serve with Sunshine: Plate up these delightful potatoes and enjoy them alongside your favorite Greek-inspired dishes, or indulge in their crispy, lemony goodness on their own.

NUTRITIONAL INFORMATION (PER SERVING, APPROXIMATE):

Calories: 250, Fat: 10g, Saturated Fat: 1g, Cholesterol: 0mg, Sodium: 200mg, Carbohydrates: 35g, Fiber: 2g, Sugar: 2g, Protein: 2g

Prep Time: 15 minutes **Cooking Time**: 15 minutes **Total Time**: 30 minutes **Servings**: 4-6

Ingredients:

FOR THE LEMONY QUINOA:

- 1 cup quinoa, rinsed
- 2 cups water
- 1/4 cup fresh lemon juice
- 1 tablespoon olive oil
- Salt and black pepper to taste

FOR THE SALAD:

- 2 cups cherry tomatoes, halved
- 1/2 cup chopped fresh parsley
- 1/4 cup chopped fresh mint
- 1/4 cup chopped fresh basil
- 1/4 cup sliced red onion (optional)
- 1/4 cup sliced almonds, toasted
- Feta cheese (optional, for crumbling)

Method:

1. Cook the Quinoa: In a medium saucepan, combine rinsed quinoa, water, lemon juice, olive oil, salt, and pepper. Bring to a boil, then reduce heat, cover, and simmer for 15 minutes, or until the quinoa is fluffy and cooked through. Fluff the quinoa with a fork and set it aside to cool slightly.

2. Prep the Salad: While the quinoa cools, slice the cherry tomatoes in half. Chop the fresh parsley, mint, and basil. Optionally, you can thinly slice the red onion and toast the almonds in a dry pan until golden brown.

3. Assemble the Salad: In a large bowl, combine the cooled quinoa, tomatoes, herbs, red onion (if using), and almonds. Season with additional salt and pepper to taste.

128

4. Optional Finishing Touches: Crumble feta cheese over the salad for a creamy and salty touch. You can also drizzle with a little extra olive oil or a squeeze of lemon juice for added brightness.

5. Serve with Sunshine: Enjoy this refreshing salad on its own, alongside grilled chicken or fish, or nestled in lettuce wraps for a light and flavorful meal.

NUTRITIONAL INFORMATION (PER SERVING, APPROXIMATE):

Calories: 250, Fat: 8g, Saturated Fat: 1g, Cholesterol: 0mg, Sodium: 150mg, Carbohydrates: 35g, Fiber: 4g, Sugar: 5g, Protein: 8g

GRILLED HALLOUMI & WATERMELON SALAD

Prep Time: 15 minutes **Cooking Time**: 10 minutes **Total Time**: 25 minutes **Servings**: 4

Ingredients:

FOR THE SALAD:

- 1/2 ripe watermelon, seeded and cut into 1-inch cubes
- 8 ounces halloumi cheese, sliced 1/2-inch thick
- 1/4 cup fresh mint leaves, chopped

FOR THE DRESSING:

- 2 tablespoons olive oil
- 1 tablespoon balsamic vinegar
- 1 teaspoon Dijon mustard
- 1/2 teaspoon honey
- Salt and black pepper to taste

Method:

1. Prep the Watermelon: Wash and dry the watermelon. Cut it in half, discard the seeds, and then cut the flesh into 1-inch cubes. Set aside.
2. Slice the Halloumi: Slice the halloumi cheese into thick (1/2-inch) slices. Pat them dry with paper towels to remove excess moisture.
3. Make the Dressing: In a small bowl, whisk together olive oil, balsamic vinegar, Dijon mustard, and honey. Season with salt and pepper to taste.
4. Grill the Halloumi: Heat a grill pan or skillet over medium heat. Lightly brush the pan with olive oil. Add the halloumi slices and cook for 2-3 minutes per side, or until golden brown and slightly crispy.
5. Assemble the Salad: In a large bowl, combine the cubed watermelon, grilled halloumi slices, and chopped mint leaves. Drizzle with the balsamic dressing and gently toss to coat.

6. Serve with Sunshine: Plate the salad and enjoy the refreshing interplay of sweet watermelon, salty halloumi, and tangy dressing.

NUTRITIONAL INFORMATION (PER SERVING, APPROXIMATE):

Calories: 250, Fat: 10g, Saturated Fat: 4g, Cholesterol: 60mg, Sodium: 300mg, Carbohydrates: 30g, Fiber: 2g, Sugar: 25g, Protein: 10g

Prep Time: 15 minutes **Cooking Time**: 20-25 minutes **Total Time**: 35-40 minutes   **Servings**: 6-8

Ingredients:

FOR THE FRITTERS:

- 1 (15-ounce) can chickpeas, drained and rinsed (can soak dried chickpeas overnight for a richer flavor)
- 1/4 cup chopped onion
- 1/4 cup chopped parsley
- 1/4 cup chopped cilantro
- 1 clove garlic, minced
- 1 teaspoon cumin
- 1/2 teaspoon coriander
- 1/4 teaspoon paprika
- 1/4 cup chickpea flour or all-purpose flour
- Salt and black pepper to taste
- Olive oil for frying

FOR THE TAHINI SAUCE:

- 1/4 cup tahini
- 2 tablespoons lemon juice
- 2 tablespoons water
- 1 clove garlic, minced
- 2 tablespoons olive oil
- Salt and black pepper to taste
- Optional Garnishes:
- Chopped fresh herbs (parsley, cilantro, mint)
- Chopped red onion
- Lemon wedges

Method:

1. Mash the Chickpeas: In a large bowl, mash the chickpeas with a fork or food processor until coarsely textured. You can leave some whole chickpeas for extra texture.
2. Add Flavor: Stir in the chopped onion, parsley, cilantro, garlic, cumin, coriander, paprika, chickpea flour, salt, and pepper. Mix well to combine.

3. Shape the Fritters: Form the mixture into small patties, about 1-1.5 inches in diameter.

4. Heat the Oil: Heat a generous amount of olive oil in a frying pan over medium heat. The oil should shimmer but not smoke.

5. Fry the Fritters: Add the fritters to the hot oil in batches and cook for 2-3 minutes per side, or until golden brown and crispy. Drain on paper towels.

6. Make the Tahini Sauce: While the fritters fry, whisk together tahini, lemon juice, water, garlic, olive oil, salt, and pepper in a small bowl until smooth. Adjust the consistency with additional water if needed.

7. Assemble and Serve: Arrange the fried fritters on a serving platter. Drizzle with tahini sauce and garnish with your chosen toppings.

NUTRITIONAL INFORMATION (PER SERVING, APPROXIMATE):

Calories: 200, Fat: 8g,, Saturated Fat: 1g, Cholesterol: 0mg, Sodium: 150mg, Carbohydrates: 20g, Fiber: 2g, Sugar: 2g, Protein: 7g

Prep Time: 15 minutes **Cooking Time**: 35-40 minutes **Total Time**: 50 minutes **Servings**: 4-6

Ingredients:

FOR THE DIP:

- 1 pound cherry tomatoes, halved
- 1/4 cup olive oil
- 1/4 cup chopped fresh oregano (or thyme)
- 2 cloves garlic, minced
- 1/2 teaspoon salt
- 1/4 teaspoon black pepper
- 8 ounces block feta cheese (preferably Greek)

FOR SERVING:

- Warm pita bread, wedges or whole
- Chopped fresh parsley, optional garnish

Method:

1. Preheat oven to 400°F (200°C). Line a baking dish with parchment paper.
2. Prep the Tomatoes: Toss the halved cherry tomatoes with olive oil, oregano, garlic, salt, and pepper in a bowl. Spread them out evenly in the prepared baking dish.
3. Nestle the Feta: Place the block of feta in the center of the tomatoes, pushing them aside slightly to create a well.
4. Roast to Perfection: Bake the tomatoes and feta for 35-40 minutes, or until the tomatoes are softened and slightly shriveled, and the feta is melty and golden brown around the edges.
5. Serve with Sunshine: Transfer the hot dip to a serving dish or leave it in the baking pan. Tear or cut the warm pita bread into wedges and offer them alongside the dip. Sprinkle with chopped parsley for an extra pop of freshness.

6. Dive In: Enjoy the creamy feta mingling with the juicy tomatoes and fragrant herbs, scooped up with warm pita bread for a taste of the Mediterranean that's simple yet utterly satisfying.

NUTRITIONAL INFORMATION (PER SERVING, APPROXIMATE):

Calories: 350, Fat: 20g, Saturated Fat: 8g, Cholesterol: 70mg, Sodium: 400mg, Carbohydrates: 30g

Fiber: 2g, Sugar: 5g, Protein: 15g

Prep Time: 15 minutes **Cooking Time**: None   **Total Time**: 15 minutes **Servings**: 4-6

Ingredients:

- 1 cup plain Greek yogurt (2% or non-fat works best)
- 1/2 cucumber, grated and drained
- 1/4 cup chopped fresh dill (or mint, for a twist)
- 1 clove garlic, minced
- 1 tablespoon olive oil
- 1/2 tablespoon lemon juice
- Salt and black pepper to taste

Method:

1. Drain the Cucumber: Grate the cucumber on the coarse side of a box grater. Place the grated cucumber in a colander and sprinkle with a pinch of salt. Let it sit for 10 minutes, then squeeze out excess moisture with your hands. This step ensures the sauce doesn't become watery.
2. Combine the Base: In a medium bowl, whisk together the Greek yogurt, drained cucumber, dill (or mint), garlic, olive oil, and lemon juice.
3. Season and Chill: Season generously with salt and pepper to taste. Cover the bowl and refrigerate for at least 30 minutes to allow the flavors to meld. The longer it chills, the better!
4. Serve with Sunshine: Your creamy Tzatziki sauce is ready to enjoy! Spoon it over grilled chicken or lamb, roasted vegetables, or use it as a dip for pita bread chips. It's also fantastic alongside falafel or as a cool topping for gyros.

NUTRITIONAL INFORMATION (PER SERVING, APPROXIMATE):

Calories: 50, Fat: 1g, Saturated Fat: 0g, Cholesterol: 2mg, Sodium: 70mg, Carbohydrates: 4g, Fiber: 0g, Sugar: 2g, Protein: 4g

Prep Time: 15 minutes **Cook Time**: 20-25 minutes **Total Time**: 40 minutes **Servings**: 4-6

Ingredients:

- 2 medium zucchinis
- 1/2 cup all-purpose flour
- 1/4 cup panko breadcrumbs
- 1/4 cup grated Parmesan cheese
- 2 tablespoons olive oil
- 1 tablespoon chopped fresh parsley

- 1 tablespoon chopped fresh basil
- 1/2 teaspoon dried oregano
- 1/4 teaspoon garlic powder
- 1/4 teaspoon salt
- 1/4 teaspoon black pepper

Method:

1. Prep the Zucchini: Wash and dry the zucchinis. Trim the ends and cut them into sticks about 1/2-inch thick and 3-4 inches long.

2. Make the Herb & Cheese Coating: In a shallow bowl, combine the flour, panko breadcrumbs, Parmesan cheese, olive oil, parsley, basil, oregano, garlic powder, salt, and pepper. Mix well to create a fragrant, crumbly mixture.

3. Coat the Zucchini Sticks: Toss the zucchini sticks in the seasoned breadcrumb mixture until evenly coated. Ensure all sides are covered.

4. Bake to Perfection: Preheat oven to 400°F (200°C). Line a baking sheet with parchment paper. Spread the coated zucchini sticks in a single layer on the prepared baking sheet.

5. Kiss them with Fire: Bake the zucchini fries for 20-25 minutes, flipping them halfway through cooking, until golden brown and crispy on the outside and tender on the inside.

6. Serve with Sunshine: Plate the fries and enjoy them hot with your favorite dipping sauce. Marinara, hummus, or even ranch dressing all pair beautifully with the garlicky, herb-infused flavor.

NUTRITIONAL INFORMATION (PER SERVING, APPROXIMATE):

Calories: 200, Fat: 8g, Saturated Fat: 1g, Cholesterol: 0mg, Sodium: 250mg, Carbohydrates: 25g, Fiber: 2g, Sugar: 3g, Protein: 5g

MARINATED ARTICHOKE HEARTS WITH OLIVES & HERBS

Prep Time: 15 minutes **Marinating Time**: Minimum 2 hours, (preferably overnight) **Total Time**: 2 hours 15 minutes (minimum) **Servings**: 4-6 (depending on portion size)

Ingredients:

- 1/2 cup sun-dried tomatoes, chopped
- 1/4 cup pitted Kalamata olives, halved
- 1/4 cup chopped fresh parsley
- 1/4 cup chopped fresh basil
- 2 tablespoons olive oil
- 1 tablespoon lemon juice

- 1 tablespoon balsamic vinegar
- 1 clove garlic, minced
- 1/2 teaspoon dried oregano
- 1/4 teaspoon red pepper flakes (optional)
- Salt and black pepper to taste

Method:

1. Whip Up the Marinade: In a medium bowl, combine the chopped sun-dried tomatoes, olives, parsley, basil, olive oil, lemon juice, balsamic vinegar, garlic, oregano, red pepper flakes (if using), salt, and pepper. Mix well to create a fragrant and flavorful mixture.
2. Meet the Artichokes: Add the drained and quartered artichoke hearts to the marinade. Gently toss to coat them evenly in the flavorful bath.
3. Embrace the Sunshine: Cover the bowl tightly and refrigerate for at least 2 hours, preferably overnight. This allows the artichokes to absorb the marinade's deliciousness.
4. Serve with Savor: When ready to serve, arrange the marinated artichoke hearts on a platter or in individual bowls. Drizzle with any extra marinade from the bottom of the bowl, and sprinkle with freshly cracked black pepper if desired.

5. Dive In: Enjoy these sun-kissed artichoke bites on their own, atop toasted baguette slices for bruschetta, or nestled alongside other antipasto favorites. Each bite is a refreshing and flavorful escape to the Mediterranean.

NUTRITIONAL INFORMATION (PER SERVING, APPROXIMATE):

Calories: 200, Fat: 10g, Saturated Fat: 1g, Cholesterol: 0mg, Sodium: 300mg, Carbohydrates: 15g, Fiber: 2g, Sugar: 5g, Protein: 4g

ROASTED BRUSSELS SPROUTS WITH BALSAMIC GLAZE & GOAT CHEESE

Prep Time: 15 minutes **Cooking Time**: 20-25 minutes **Total Time**: 35-40 minutes **Servings: 4-6**

Ingredients:

- 1 pound Brussels sprouts, trimmed and halved
- 1 tablespoon olive oil
- 1/2 teaspoon salt
- 1/4 teaspoon black pepper

- For the Balsamic Glaze:
- 1/4 cup balsamic vinegar
- 1 tablespoon honey or brown sugar
- 1/2 teaspoon Dijon mustard

Method:

1. Preheat the Oven: Crank your oven to 400°F (200°C). Line a baking sheet with parchment paper for easy cleanup.

2. Prep the Brussels Sprouts: Wash and trim the Brussels sprouts. Cut them in half lengthwise, ensuring they are roughly equal in size for even cooking.

3. Toss & Coat: In a large bowl, toss the halved Brussels sprouts with olive oil, salt, and pepper until evenly coated. Spread them out in a single layer on the prepared baking sheet.

4. Kiss them with Fire: Roast the Brussels sprouts for 20-25 minutes, flipping them halfway through cooking, until they are golden brown and crispy on the edges and tender inside.

5. Whip Up the Glaze: While the Brussels sprouts roast, heat the balsamic vinegar, honey or brown sugar, and Dijon mustard in a small saucepan over medium heat. Bring to a simmer and cook until the mixture thickens and reduces by half, about 5-7 minutes. Set aside.

6. Dress to Impress: Drizzle the roasted Brussels sprouts with the balsamic glaze, tossing gently to coat them evenly.

7. Goat Cheese Bliss: Sprinkle the crumbled goat cheese over the glazed Brussels sprouts. Garnish with chopped parsley, if desired.

8. Serve with Sunshine: Plate these savory-sweet delights and enjoy them alongside your favorite dishes, or indulge in them solo.

NUTRITIONAL INFORMATION (PER SERVING, APPROXIMATE):

Calories: 200, Fat: 10g, Saturated Fat: 2g, Cholesterol: 10mg, Sodium: 150mg, Carbohydrates: 25g, Fiber: 4g, Sugar: 10g, Protein: 5g

Prep Time: 10 minutes **Cooking Time**: 20 minutes **Total Time:** 30 minutes **Servings**: 4-6

Ingredients:

- 2 cups long-grain rice (basmati or jasmine works well)
- 2 tablespoons olive oil
- 1 onion, finely chopped
- 1 garlic clove, minced
- 1/2 cup chicken broth (vegetable broth works for a vegetarian option)
- 1 1/2 cups water
- 1/4 cup freshly squeezed lemon juice (about 1 lemon)
- 1/4 teaspoon salt
- 1/4 teaspoon black pepper
- 1/4 cup chopped fresh parsley, optional garnish

Method:

1. Heat the Oil: In a large saucepan or pot, heat olive oil over medium heat. Add the chopped onion and cook until softened and translucent, about 5 minutes.
2. Toast the Rice: Stir in the rice and cook for a minute, stirring constantly, until the grains are coated in oil and slightly translucent. This step enhances the rice flavor and texture.
3. Add the Liquids: Pour in the chicken broth and water. Stir in the lemon juice, salt, and pepper. Bring to a boil, then reduce heat to low, cover the pot tightly, and simmer for 20 minutes, or until the rice is cooked through and all the liquid is absorbed.
4. Fluff and Finish: Remove the pot from heat and let it sit covered for 5 minutes. This allows the flavors to meld and the rice to fluff up further. Fluff the rice gently with a fork before serving.
5. Serve with Sunshine: Spoon the fluffy rice onto plates and garnish with chopped fresh parsley, if desired. This lemony pilaf is the perfect accompaniment to grilled chicken, lamb, roasted vegetables, or even enjoyed solo as a light and flavorful meal.

NUTRITIONAL INFORMATION (PER SERVING, APPROXIMATE) :

Calories: 200, Fat: 5g, Saturated Fat: 1g, Cholesterol: 0mg, Sodium: 150mg, Carbohydrates: 35g, Fiber: 1g, Sugar: 2g, Protein: 3g

NUTRITIONAL INFORMATION (PER SERVING, APPROXIMATE) :

CHAPTER EIGHT

POULTRY

81. LEMON ROSEMARY ROAST CHICKEN WITH CRISPY POTATOES

82. SPICED MOROCCAN CHICKEN TAGINE WITH PRUNES AND ALMONDS

83. GREEK CHICKEN KEBABS WITH LEMON & OREGANO, GRILLED VEGETABLES & TZATZIKI

84. CHICKEN & CHORIZO SKEWERS WITH ROASTED PEPPERS AND ONIONS

85. CRISPY PAN-SEARED DUCK BREAST WITH FIG & ORANGE SAUCE

86. TURKISH SPICED GRILLED CHICKEN WINGS WITH YOGURT MARINADE

87. HONEY GARLIC CHICKEN SALAD WITH GRAPES AND FETA

88. LEMON HERB STUFFED CHICKEN BREASTS WITH ROASTED VEGETABLES.

89. TUSCAN CHICKEN WITH WHITE BEANS & KALE

90. GREEK CHICKEN GYROS WITH TZATZIKI SAUCE

Prep Time: 15 minutes **Cooking Time**: 1 hour 20 minutes **Total Time**: 1 hour 35 minutes **Servings**: 4-6

Ingredients:

FOR THE CHICKEN:

- 1 whole roasting chicken (around 4-5 pounds)
- 1 tablespoon olive oil
- 1 lemon, quartered
- 2 sprigs fresh rosemary
- 1/2 teaspoon salt
- 1/4 teaspoon black pepper

FOR THE CRISPY POTATOES:

- 1 pound potatoes (Yukon Gold work well)
- 2 tablespoons olive oil
- 1/2 teaspoon salt
- 1/4 teaspoon black pepper

Method:

1. Preheat the Oven: Crank your oven to 425°F (220°C).
2. Prep the Chicken: Pat the chicken dry with paper towels. Drizzle with olive oil and massage it over the skin to coat evenly.
3. Infuse with Flavor: Tuck lemon quarters and rosemary sprigs inside the chicken cavity. Season generously with salt and pepper.
4. Tie it Up: Using kitchen twine, tie the legs together to keep the bird compact for even cooking.
5. Gather the Troops: Place the chicken on a roasting rack set over a baking sheet. Arrange the potatoes, cut into halves or wedges, around the chicken on the baking sheet.
6. Drizzle & Season: Drizzle the potatoes with olive oil and toss to coat. Season with salt and pepper.

7. Kiss them with Fire: Roast the chicken and potatoes for 1 hour and 10 minutes, flipping the potatoes halfway through cooking. For a deeper golden brown on the chicken, baste it with the pan drippings in the last 10 minutes.

8. Rest for Perfection: Transfer the chicken to a cutting board and let it rest for 10 minutes before carving. This allows the juices to redistribute, ensuring moist and flavorful meat.

9. Serve with Sunshine: Plate the sliced chicken and crispy potatoes, drizzled with any pan drippings, for a feast fit for the senses.

NUTRITIONAL INFORMATION (PER SERVING, APPROXIMATE):

Calories: 50, Fat: 25g, Saturated Fat: 5g, Cholesterol: 200mg, Sodium: 400mg

Carbohydrates: 50g, Fiber: 4g, Sugar: 5g Protein: 40g

SPICED MOROCCAN CHICKEN TAGINE WITH PRUNES AND ALMONDS

Prep Time: 15 minutes **Cooking Time**: 1 hour 15 minutes **Total Time**: 1 hour 30 minutes **Servings**: 4-6

Ingredients:

FOR THE CHICKEN:

- 1 tablespoon olive oil
- 1 whole chicken (around 3-4 pounds), cut into 8 pieces
- 1 onion, chopped
- 2 cloves garlic, minced
- 1 teaspoon ground ginger
- 1/2 teaspoon turmeric
- 1/2 teaspoon cinnamon
- 1/4 teaspoon cayenne pepper (adjust to your spice preference)
- 1/4 teaspoon saffron (optional)
- 1/2 teaspoon salt
- 1/4 teaspoon black pepper

FOR THE SAUCE:

- 1 (14.5-ounce) can diced tomatoes, undrained
- 1/2 cup chicken broth
- 1/4 cup pitted prunes, chopped
- 1/4 cup blanched almonds, toasted and roughly chopped
- 1 tablespoon honey
- 1/2 teaspoon coriander seeds, crushed
- Fresh cilantro, chopped, for garnish (optional)

Method:

1. Heat the Pot: In a large tagine or Dutch oven, heat olive oil over medium heat.

2. Brown the Chicken: Season the chicken pieces with salt and pepper. Add them to the hot oil and sear until golden brown on all sides.

3. Build the Flavor Base: Remove the chicken and set it aside. Add the chopped onion to the pot and cook until softened and translucent. Stir in the garlic, ginger, turmeric, cinnamon, cayenne pepper, and saffron (if using). Cook for 30 seconds, releasing the fragrant spices.

4. Simmer in Goodness: Pour in the diced tomatoes and chicken broth. Scrape up any browned bits from the bottom of the pot to add flavor. Return the chicken pieces to the pot, nestling them in the sauce.

5. Sweeten and Spice: Stir in the chopped prunes, toasted almonds, honey, and crushed coriander seeds. Bring to a simmer, then reduce heat to low, cover the pot, and cook for 1 hour, or until the chicken is cooked through and tender.

6. Taste of Morocco: When the chicken is cooked, taste the sauce and adjust seasonings with salt and pepper if needed. Garnish with chopped cilantro (optional) and serve with fluffy couscous or crusty bread for soaking up the flavorful sauce.

NUTRITIONAL INFORMATION (PER SERVING, APPROXIMATE):

Calories: 450, Fat: 20g, Saturated Fat: 4g, Cholesterol: 120mg, Sodium: 450mg, Carbohydrates: 40g, Fiber: 4g, Sugar: 15g, Protein: 40g

GREEK CHICKEN KEBABS WITH LEMON & OREGANO, GRILLED VEGETABLES & TZATZIKI

Prep Time: 15 minutes (plus marinating time, minimum 30 minutes) **Cook Time**: 15-20 minutes **Total Time**: 45 minutes (minimum) **Servings**: 4-6

Ingredients:

FOR THE CHICKEN KEBABS:

- 1 pound boneless, skinless chicken breasts or thighs, cut into 1-inch cubes
- 1/4 cup olive oil
- 2 tablespoons lemon juice
- 1 tablespoon dried oregano
- 1 teaspoon garlic powder
- 1/2 teaspoon salt
- 1/4 teaspoon black pepper
- 1 red bell pepper, cut into chunks
- 1 green bell pepper, cut into chunks
- 1 zucchini, cut into chunks
- 1 red onion, cut into wedges
- Wooden skewers (soaked in water for at least 30 minutes to prevent burning)

Method:

1. Marinate the Chicken: In a large bowl, combine the olive oil, lemon juice, oregano, garlic powder, salt, and pepper. Add the chicken cubes and toss to coat evenly. Cover and refrigerate for at least 30 minutes, or up to overnight, for deeper flavor.
2. Skewer the Goodness: Thread the marinated chicken cubes onto pre-soaked wooden skewers, alternating with chunks of bell peppers, zucchini, and red onion.
3. Fire Up the Grill: Preheat your grill to medium-high heat.
4. Kiss them with Flame: Grill the skewers for 15-20 minutes, turning occasionally, until the chicken is cooked through and vegetables are tender-crisp.
5. Whip Up the Tzatziki: While the skewers grill, prepare the Tzatziki sauce. Grate the cucumber and place it in a colander. Sprinkle with a pinch of salt and let it drain for 10 minutes. Squeeze out any

excess moisture. In a bowl, combine the drained cucumber with yogurt, dill (or mint), garlic, olive oil, lemon juice, salt, and pepper. Mix well and refrigerate until serving.

6. Serve with Sunshine: Plate the grilled skewers and drizzle with any remaining marinade if desired. Serve alongside the cool and refreshing Tzatziki sauce, offering pita bread or flatbreads for scooping up the deliciousness.

NUTRITIONAL INFORMATION (PER SERVING, APPROXIMATE):

Calories: 350, Fat: 15g, Saturated Fat: 3g, Cholesterol: 80mg, Sodium: 350mg, Carbohydrates: 25g, Fiber: 2g, Sugar: 5g, Protein: 30g

CHICKEN & CHORIZO SKEWERS WITH ROASTED PEPPERS AND ONIONS

Prep Time: 15 minutes **Cooking Time**: 20-25 minutes **Total Time**: 35-40 minutes **Servings:** 4-6

Ingredients:

- For the Skewers:
- 1 pound boneless, skinless chicken breasts or thighs, cut into 1-inch cubes
- 8 ounces chorizo sausage, sliced into 1-inch pieces
- 1 red bell pepper, cut into chunks
- 1 yellow bell pepper, cut into chunks
- 1 red onion, cut into wedges
- 1 tablespoon olive oil
- 1 teaspoon smoked paprika
- 1/2 teaspoon dried oregano
- 1/2 teaspoon garlic powder
- 1/4 teaspoon salt
- 1/4 teaspoon black pepper
- Wooden skewers (soaked in water for at least 30 minutes to prevent burning)

Method:

1. Make the Spice Mix: In a small bowl, combine the olive oil, paprika, oregano, garlic powder, salt, and pepper.
2. Marinate the Meat: In a large bowl, toss the chicken and chorizo cubes with the spiced olive oil mixture. Cover and refrigerate for at least 20 minutes, or up to overnight, for deeper flavor.
3. Assemble the Skewers: Thread the marinated chicken, chorizo, peppers, and onion onto pre-soaked wooden skewers, alternating for visual appeal.
4. Fire Up the Grill: Preheat your grill to medium-high heat.
5. Kiss them with Flame: Grill the skewers for 20-25 minutes, turning occasionally, until the chicken is cooked through, the chorizo is slightly crispy, and the vegetables are tender-crisp.
6. Serve with Sizzle: Plate the grilled skewers and enjoy them hot with your favorite accompaniments like crusty bread, chimichurri sauce, yogurt dip, or a sprinkling of fresh parsley.

NUTRITIONAL INFORMATION (PER SERVING, APPROXIMATE):

Calories: 400, Fat: 20g, Saturated Fat: 5g, Cholesterol: 80mg, Sodium: 400mg, Carbohydrates: 25g, Fiber: 2g, Sugar: 5g, Protein: 35g

Prep Time: 15 minutes **Cooking Time**: 20-25 minutes **Total Time**: 35-40 minutes **Servings**: 2-3

Ingredients:

FOR THE DUCK BREASTS:

- 2 duck breasts (8-10 ounces each), skin on, trimmed of excess fat
- 1 tablespoon olive oil
- 1/2 teaspoon salt
- 1/4 teaspoon black pepper
- For the Fig & Orange Sauce:
- 1 tablespoon olive oil
- 1 shallot, finely chopped
- 1/2 cup dry red wine
- 1/4 cup chicken broth
- 1/4 cup fresh orange juice
- 1/4 cup dried figs, chopped
- 1 tablespoon fig jam
- 1/2 teaspoon grated orange zest
- 1/4 teaspoon dried thyme
- Salt and black pepper to taste

Method:

1. Score the Duck: Using a sharp knife, lightly score the duck skin in a criss-cross pattern, taking care not to pierce the meat. This allows the fat to render and the skin to crisp up beautifully.
2. Season & Sizzle: Pat the duck breasts dry with paper towels and season generously with salt and pepper. Heat olive oil in a large ovenproof skillet over medium-high heat. Once hot, place the duck breasts skin-side down and sear for 5-7 minutes, until the skin is golden brown and crispy.
3. Flip & Finish: Flip the duck breasts and reduce heat to medium. Cook for another 5-7 minutes, or until the duck reaches your desired doneness (medium-rare is recommended for optimal tenderness). Transfer the duck breasts to a plate and cover loosely with foil to rest.
4. Simmer the Sauce: In the same skillet, add the remaining olive oil and shallot. Sauté until softened and translucent, about 3 minutes. Pour in the red wine, chicken broth, and orange juice. Bring to a simmer and cook until reduced by half, about 5 minutes.

5. Sweeten & Spice: Stir in the chopped figs, fig jam, orange zest, and thyme. Season with salt and pepper to taste. Simmer for another 3 minutes, allowing the flavors to meld.

6. Plate with Perfection: Return the duck breasts to the pan and baste with the fig and orange sauce for a minute. Plate the duck breasts, drizzle with more sauce, and garnish with fresh thyme sprigs if desired. Serve alongside mashed potatoes or roasted root vegetables for a complete and delectable meal.

NUTRITIONAL INFORMATION (PER SERVING, APPROXIMATE):

Calories: 600, Fat: 40g, Saturated Fat: 10g, Cholesterol: 150mg, Sodium: 400mg, Carbohydrates: 30g, Fiber: 4g, Sugar: 15g, Protein: 50g

TURKISH SPICED GRILLED CHICKEN WINGS WITH YOGURT MARINADE

Prep Time: 15 minutes (plus marinating time, minimum 30 minutes) **Cooking Time**: 20-25 minutes **Total Time**: 45 minutes (minimum) **Servings**: 4-6

Ingredients:

FOR THE CHICKEN WINGS:

- 1 pound chicken wings, separated at the joint
- 1/4 cup plain Greek yogurt
- 2 tablespoons olive oil
- 1 tablespoon lemon juice
- 1 tablespoon Turkish hot pepper paste (biber salcasi)
- 1 teaspoon garlic powder
- 1/2 teaspoon dried oregano
- 1/2 teaspoon cumin
- 1/4 teaspoon smoked paprika
- 1/4 teaspoon salt
- 1/4 teaspoon black pepper

FOR SERVING (OPTIONAL):

- Yogurt dip (plain Greek yogurt mixed with lemon juice, garlic, and herbs)
- Chopped fresh parsley
- Lemon wedges

Method:

1. Mix the Spice Blend: In a large bowl, whisk together the yogurt, olive oil, lemon juice, pepper paste, garlic powder, oregano, cumin, paprika, salt, and pepper. This aromatic marinade is the heart of the flavor symphony.
2. Coat the Wings: Add the chicken wings to the bowl and toss them well to coat evenly in the spiced yogurt marinade. Cover and refrigerate for at least 30 minutes, or up to overnight, for deeper flavor infusion.
3. Fire Up the Grill: Preheat your grill to medium-high heat.

4. Kiss them with Flame: Arrange the marinated wings on the preheated grill. Grill for 20-25 minutes, turning occasionally, until cooked through and browned with slightly crispy skin. The flames will kiss the wings with smoky goodness.
5. Serve with Sizzle: Plate the grilled wings hot and drizzle with additional marinade if desired. Offer creamy yogurt dip, chopped parsley, and lemon wedges for a complete and refreshing experience.

NUTRITIONAL INFORMATION (PER SERVING, APPROXIMATE):

Calories: 350, Fat: 20g, Saturated Fat: 3g, Cholesterol: 80mg, Sodium: 400mg, Carbohydrates: 5g

Fiber: 1g, Sugar: 2g, Protein: 35g

Prep Time: 10 minutes **Cooking Time**: 15 minutes **Total Time**: 25 minutes **Servings**: 2-3

Ingredients:

FOR THE CHICKEN:

- 1 pound boneless, skinless chicken breasts or thighs, cut into bite-sized pieces
- 1 tablespoon olive oil
- 1 tablespoon soy sauce
- 1 tablespoon honey
- 1 tablespoon minced garlic
- 1/2 teaspoon salt
- 1/4 teaspoon black pepper

FOR THE SALAD:

- 4 cups mixed greens (baby spinach, arugula, and romaine work well)
- 1 cup red grapes, halved
- 1/2 cup crumbled feta cheese
- 1/4 cup sliced almonds (optional)
- For the Dressing (optional):
- 2 tablespoons olive oil
- 1 tablespoon lemon juice
- 1 teaspoon honey
- 1/2 teaspoon Dijon mustard
- Salt and pepper to taste

Method:

1. Marinate the Chicken: In a medium bowl, whisk together the olive oil, soy sauce, honey, garlic, salt, and pepper. Add the chicken pieces and toss to coat evenly. Marinate for at least 10 minutes for deeper flavor.

2. Cook the Chicken: Heat a large skillet or grill pan over medium-high heat. Add the marinated chicken and cook for 5-7 minutes per side, or until cooked through and golden brown. Transfer the cooked chicken to a plate and let it cool slightly.

3. Assemble the Salad: In a large bowl, toss the mixed greens with the grapes, feta cheese, and almonds (if using).
4. Dress to Impress: If using, whisk together the olive oil, lemon juice, honey, and Dijon mustard in a small bowl. Drizzle the dressing over the salad to your desired amount.
5. Top it Off: Top the dressed salad with the cooled chicken pieces.

NUTRITIONAL INFORMATION (PER SERVING, APPROXIMATE):

Calories: 400, Fat: 15g, Saturated Fat: 3g, Cholesterol: 80mg, Sodium: 400mg, Carbohydrates: 25g, Fiber: 2g, Sugar: 15g, Protein: 35g

LEMON HERB STUFFED CHICKEN BREASTS WITH ROASTED VEGETABLES.

Prep Time: 10 minutes **Cooking Time**: 15 minutes **Total Time**: 25 minutes **Servings**: 2-3

Ingredients:

FOR THE CHICKEN:

- 1 pound boneless, skinless chicken breasts or thighs, cut into bite-sized pieces
- 1 tablespoon olive oil
- 1 tablespoon soy sauce
- 1 tablespoon honey
- 1 tablespoon minced garlic
- 1/2 teaspoon salt
- 1/4 teaspoon black pepper
- For the Salad:
- 4 cups mixed greens (baby spinach, arugula, and romaine work well)
- 1 cup red grapes, halved
- 1/2 cup crumbled feta cheese
- 1/4 cup sliced almonds (optional)

FOR THE DRESSING (OPTIONAL):

- 2 tablespoons olive oil
- 1 tablespoon lemon juice
- 1 teaspoon honey
- 1/2 teaspoon Dijon mustard
- Salt and pepper to taste

Method:

1. Marinate the Chicken: In a medium bowl, whisk together the olive oil, soy sauce, honey, garlic, salt, and pepper. Add the chicken pieces and toss to coat evenly. Marinate for at least 10 minutes for deeper flavor.

2. Cook the Chicken: Heat a large skillet or grill pan over medium-high heat. Add the marinated chicken and cook for 5-7 minutes per side, or until cooked through and golden brown. Transfer the cooked chicken to a plate and let it cool slightly.

3. Assemble the Salad: In a large bowl, toss the mixed greens with the grapes, feta cheese, and almonds (if using).

4. Dress to Impress: If using, whisk together the olive oil, lemon juice, honey, and Dijon mustard in a small bowl. Drizzle the dressing over the salad to your desired amount.

5. Top it Off: Top the dressed salad with the cooled chicken pieces. Enjoy immediately!

NUTRITIONAL INFORMATION (PER SERVING, APPROXIMATE):

Calories: 400, Fat: 15g, Saturated Fat: 3g, Cholesterol: 80mg, Sodium: 400mg, Carbohydrates: 25g, Fiber: 2g, Sugar: 15g, Protein: 35g

Prep Time: 15 minutes **Cooking Time**: 1 hour **Total Time**: 1 hour 15 minutes **Servings**: 4-6

Ingredients:

FOR THE CHICKEN:

- 1 tablespoon olive oil
- 1 pound boneless, skinless chicken thighs, cut into bite-sized pieces
- 1/2 teaspoon salt
- 1/4 teaspoon black pepper

FOR THE SAUCE:

- 2 ounces pancetta, chopped (optional)
- 1 onion, chopped
- 2 cloves garlic, minced
- 1 (28-ounce) can diced tomatoes, undrained
- 1/2 cup chicken broth
- 1/4 cup sun-dried tomatoes, chopped
- 1 (15-ounce) can cannellini beans, drained and rinsed
- 1 bunch kale, stemmed and roughly chopped
- 1 tablespoon chopped fresh rosemary or thyme
- 1/4 teaspoon red pepper flakes (adjust to your spice preference)
- Salt and pepper to taste

Method:

- Brown the Chicken: Heat olive oil in a large Dutch oven or ovenproof pot over medium-high heat. Season the chicken pieces with salt and pepper, then add them to the pot and cook until golden brown on all sides.

- Build the Flavor Base: Remove the chicken from the pot and set it aside. Add the pancetta (if using) and cook until crispy. Add the chopped onion and cook until softened, about 5 minutes. Stir in the garlic and cook for 30 seconds, releasing the fragrant aroma.

- Simmer in Goodness: Pour in the diced tomatoes, chicken broth, sun-dried tomatoes, cannellini beans, and kale. Bring to a simmer, then return the chicken pieces to the pot.

- Let the Flavors Mingle: Stir in the rosemary or thyme, red pepper flakes (if using), and additional salt and pepper to taste. Cover the pot and simmer for 30-40 minutes, or until the chicken is cooked through and the kale is tender.

- Taste of Tuscany: When the stew is ready, adjust seasonings if needed. Serve hot with crusty bread for soaking up the rich sauce, and enjoy a taste of Tuscan sunshine amidst your own kitchen.

NUTRITIONAL INFORMATION (PER SERVING, APPROXIMATE):

Calories: 450, Fat: 20g, Saturated Fat: 4g, Cholesterol: 120mg, Sodium: 450mg, Carbohydrates: 40g, Fiber: 4g, Sugar: 15g, Protein: 40g

GREEK CHICKEN GYROS WITH TZATZIKI SAUCE

Prep Time: 15 minutes (plus marinating time, minimum 30 minutes) **Cooking Time:** 15-20 minutes
Total Time: 45 minutes (minimum) **Servings**: 4-6 (depending on appetites)

Ingredients:

FOR THE CHICKEN GYROS:

- 1 pound boneless, skinless chicken breasts or thighs, cut into 1-inch cubes
- 1/4 cup olive oil
- 3 tablespoons lemon juice
- 2 tablespoons chopped fresh oregano
- 1 tablespoon minced garlic
- 1 teaspoon dried thyme
- 1/2 teaspoon salt
- 1/4 teaspoon black pepper
- 1 red bell pepper, cut into chunks
- 1 green bell pepper, cut into chunks
- 1 red onion, cut into wedges
- Wooden skewers (soaked in water for at least 30 minutes to prevent burning)

FOR THE TZATZIKI SAUCE:

- 1 cup plain Greek yogurt (2% or non-fat works best)
- 1/2 cucumber, grated and drained
- 1 tablespoon chopped fresh dill (or mint, for a twist)
- 1 clove garlic, minced
- 1 tablespoon olive oil
- 1/2 tablespoon lemon juice
- Salt and black pepper to tas

Method:

1. Marinate the Chicken: In a large bowl, combine the olive oil, lemon juice, oregano, garlic, thyme, salt, and pepper. Add the chicken cubes and toss to coat evenly. Cover and refrigerate for at least 30 minutes, or up to overnight, for deeper flavor.

2. Skewer the Goodness: Thread the marinated chicken cubes onto pre-soaked wooden skewers, alternating with chunks of bell peppers and onion.

3. Fire Up the Grill: Preheat your grill to medium-high heat.

4. Kiss them with Flame: Grill the skewers for 15-20 minutes, turning occasionally, until the chicken is cooked through and vegetables are tender-crisp.

5. Whip Up the Tzatziki: While the skewers grill, prepare the Tzatziki sauce. Grate the cucumber and place it in a colander. Sprinkle with a pinch of salt and let it drain for 10 minutes. Squeeze out any excess moisture. In a bowl, combine the drained cucumber with yogurt, dill (or mint), garlic, olive oil, lemon juice, salt, and pepper. Mix well and refrigerate until serving.

6. Serve with Sunshine: Plate the grilled skewers and drizzle with any remaining marinade if desired. Serve alongside the cool and refreshing Tzatziki sauce, offering pita bread or flatbreads for scooping up the deliciousness. Add chopped tomatoes, red onion, olives, and feta cheese for extra Mediterranean flair.

NUTRITIONAL INFORMATION (PER SERVING, APPROXIMATE) :

Calories: 350, Fat: 15g, Saturated Fat: 3g, Cholesterol: 80mg, Sodium: 350mg, Carbohydrates: 25g

Fiber: 2g, Sugar: 5g, Protein: 30g

CHAPTER NINE

SEA FOOD

91. MEDITERRANEAN TUNA WRAPS WITH TAHINI SAUCE & GRILLED VEGETABLES

92. GRILLED SWORDFISH WITH LEMON & CAPERS

93. PAN-SEARED SCALLOPS WITH SAFFRON RISOTTO & FENNEL

94. CRUSTED CALAMARI WITH SPICY ROMESCO SAUCE

95. MEDITERRANEAN SEAFOOD SOUP WITH SAFFRON & FENNEL

MEDITERRANEAN TUNA WRAPS WITH TAHINI SAUCE & GRILLED VEGETABLES

Prep Time: 15 minutes **Cooking Time**: 15 minutes (plus grilling time for vegetables) **Total Time**: 30 minutes Servings: 4-6 wraps

Ingredients:

FOR THE WRAPS:

- 2 cans (12 oz each) canned tuna, drained and flaked
- 1 red bell pepper, sliced
- 1 zucchini, sliced
- 1 red onion, sliced
- 1/2 cup crumbled feta cheese
- 1/4 cup chopped fresh parsley
- 6 large tortillas (whole wheat or spinach work well)

FOR THE TAHINI SAUCE:

- 1/4 cup tahini
- 1/4 cup plain Greek yogurt
- 2 tablespoons lemon juice
- 1 tablespoon olive oil
- 1 clove garlic, minced
- 1/4 teaspoon salt
- 1/4 teaspoon black pepper
- Water (optional)

Method:

1. Grill the Veggies: Preheat your grill or grill pan to medium-high heat. Grill the bell pepper, zucchini, and onion slices until tender-crisp and slightly charred, about 5-7 minutes per side.
2. Make the Tahini Sauce: In a small bowl, whisk together the tahini, yogurt, lemon juice, olive oil, garlic, salt, and pepper. Add water a tablespoon at a time until you reach a desired consistency (thicker for dipping, thinner for drizzling).

3. Assemble the Wraps: Spread a layer of tahini sauce on each tortilla. Top with flaked tuna, grilled vegetables, crumbled feta cheese, and chopped parsley.

4. Wrap it Up: Fold the bottom edge of the tortilla over the filling, then fold in the sides and roll up tightly.

NUTRITIONAL INFORMATION (PER WRAP, APPROXIMATE) :

Calories: 350, Fat: 15g, Saturated Fat: 3g, Cholesterol: 50mg, Sodium: 400mg, Carbohydrates: 30g

Fiber: 3g, Sugar: 5g, Protein: 25g

GRILLED SWORDFISH WITH LEMON & CAPERS

Prep Time: 15 minutes **Cooking Time**: 10-12 minutes **Total Time**: 25 minutes **Servings**: 2-3

Ingredients:

FOR THE SWORDFISH:

- 2 swordfish steaks (6-8 ounces each), about 1-inch thick
- 1 tablespoon olive oil

- 1/2 teaspoon salt
- 1/4 teaspoon black pepper

FOR THE LEMON & CAPER SAUCE:

- 2 tablespoons butter
- 1 tablespoon olive oil
- 1 shallot, finely chopped
- 1/4 cup dry white wine
- 1/4 cup chicken broth

- 1/4 cup fresh lemon juice
- 2 tablespoons capers, drained
- 1/4 teaspoon salt
- 1/4 teaspoon black pepper
- Chopped fresh parsley, for garnish (optional)

Method:

1. Prep the Fish: Pat the swordfish steaks dry with paper towels. Brush both sides with olive oil and season generously with salt and pepper.
2. Fire Up the Grill: Preheat your grill to medium-high heat. Alternatively, heat a large grill pan over medium-high heat.
3. Kiss with Flame: Grill the swordfish steaks for 4-5 minutes per side, or until cooked through and slightly charred. Aim for an internal temperature of 130°F (54°C) for medium-rare.
4. Whip Up the Sauce: While the fish grills, melt the butter and olive oil in a small saucepan over medium heat. Add the shallot and cook until softened, about 3 minutes. Pour in the white wine and chicken

broth, and bring to a simmer. Stir in the lemon juice, capers, salt, and pepper. Let the sauce simmer for 5 minutes to meld the flavors.

5. Plate with Perfection: Transfer the grilled swordfish steaks to serving plates. Drizzle generously with the warm lemon and caper sauce. Garnish with chopped parsley if desired, and serve with your favorite sides like grilled asparagus, roasted potatoes, or a light salad.

Nutritional Information (per serving, approximate):

Calories: 450, Fat: 30g, Saturated Fat: 10g, Cholesterol: 120mg, Sodium: 400mg, Carbohydrates: 5g, Fiber: 1g, Sugar: 2g, Protein: 50g

Prep Time: 15 minutes **Cooking Time**: 35-40 minutes **Total Time**: 50 minutes **Servings**: 2-3

Ingredients:

FOR THE SCALLOPS:

- 8 large sea scallops (dry or wet-packed)
- 1 tablespoon olive oil
- 1/2 teaspoon salt
- 1/4 teaspoon black pepper

FOR THE SAFFRON RISOTTO:

- 1 tablespoon olive oil
- 1 shallot, finely chopped
- 1 1/2 cups Arborio rice
- 1/2 cup dry white wine
- 4 cups hot chicken broth (divided)
- Pinch of saffron threads
- 1/4 cup grated Parmesan cheese
- Salt and black pepper to taste

FOR THE FENNEL:

- 1 bulb fennel, thinly sliced
- 1 tablespoon olive oil
- 1/4 cup dry white wine
- Salt and black pepper to taste

Method:

- Prep the Scallops: Pat the scallops dry with paper towels. Season generously with salt and pepper.

- Sauté the Fennel: Heat olive oil in a large skillet over medium heat. Add the fennel and cook for 5-7 minutes, until softened and slightly golden. Pour in the white wine and simmer for 2 minutes, allowing the flavors to meld. Season with salt and pepper. Set aside.

- Start the Risotto: In a separate pot, heat olive oil over medium heat. Add the shallot and cook until softened, about 3 minutes. Stir in the Arborio rice and toast for 1 minute.

- Deglaze with Wine: Pour in the white wine and cook until almost completely absorbed.

- Saffron Magic: Add a pinch of saffron threads to the hot chicken broth. Gradually add the saffron-infused broth to the rice, one ladleful at a time, stirring constantly. Let each ladleful be absorbed before adding the next. This takes about 20 minutes.

- Creamy Perfection: When the rice is al dente and the risotto is creamy, stir in the Parmesan cheese and season with salt and pepper to taste.

- Sear the Scallops: While the risotto finishes, heat a large skillet over medium-high heat with the remaining olive oil. Sear the scallops for 2-3 minutes per side, until golden brown and cooked through.

- Plate with Perfection: Spoon the creamy saffron risotto onto plates. Top with the sautéed fennel and pan-seared scallops.

NUTRITIONAL INFORMATION (PER SERVING, APPROXIMATE):

Calories: 600, Fat: 40g, Saturated Fat: 10g, Cholesterol: 150mg, Sodium: 400mg, Carbohydrates: 30g, Fiber: 4g, Sugar: 5g, Protein: 50g

CRUSTED CALAMARI WITH SPICY ROMESCO SAUCE

Prep Time: 20 minutes **Cookimg Time**: 15 minutes **Total Time**: 35 minutes **Servings**: 4-6

Ingredients:

FOR THE CALAMARI:

- 1 pound fresh or frozen calamari rings, thawed and patted dry
- 1/2 cup all-purpose flour
- 1/4 teaspoon salt
- 1/4 teaspoon black pepper

- 1 egg, beaten
- 1/2 cup panko breadcrumbs
- 1/4 cup grated Parmesan cheese
- 1/4 teaspoon paprika
- Vegetable oil for frying

FOR THE SPICY ROMESCO SAUCE:

- 1 red bell pepper, roasted and peeled (skin can be charred under broiler)
- 2 Roma tomatoes, roasted and peeled
- 1/4 cup roasted almonds
- 2 cloves garlic
- 1/4 cup tomato paste

- 2 tablespoons sherry vinegar
- 1 tablespoon smoked paprika
- 1 teaspoon chili flakes (adjust to your spice preference)
- 1/4 cup olive oil
- Salt and black pepper to taste

Method:

- Prep the Calamari: If using frozen, thaw the calamari rings and cut them into 1-inch pieces. Pat them dry with paper towels. In a shallow bowl, combine the flour, salt, and pepper. In another bowl, whisk the egg. In a third bowl, mix the panko breadcrumbs, Parmesan cheese, and paprika.

- Dredge and Coat: Dredge each calamari piece in the flour mixture, then dip it in the egg, and finally coat it evenly with the panko mixture. Shake off any excess crumbs.
- Heat the Oil: Heat a deep fryer or a large pot with enough vegetable oil to reach a depth of 1-inch to 350°F (177°C).
- Fry to Perfection: Working in batches, fry the calamari for 2-3 minutes per side, or until golden brown and crispy. Drain on paper towels to remove excess oil.
- Whip Up the Romesco: While the calamari fries, blend the roasted red pepper, tomatoes, almonds, garlic, tomato paste, sherry vinegar, paprika, chili flakes, and olive oil in a food processor until smooth. Season with salt and pepper to taste.
- Plate with Passion: Serve the crispy calamari alongside the vibrant romesco sauce for dipping. Garnish with chopped parsley or lemon wedges if desired.

NUTRITIONAL INFORMATION (PER SERVING, APPROXIMATE) :

Calories: 350, Fat: 20g, Saturated Fat: 3g, Cholesterol: 80mg, Sodium: 400mg, Carbohydrates: 25g, Fiber: 1g, Sugar: 5g, Protein: 30g

MEDITERRANEAN SEAFOOD SOUP WITH SAFFRON & FENNEL

Prep Time: 20 minutes **Cooking Time**: 45 minutes **Total Time**: 1 hour 5 minutes **Servings**: 4-6

Ingredients:

FOR THE SOUP:

- 2 tablespoons olive oil
- 1 onion, chopped
- 2 cloves garlic, minced
- 1 fennel bulb, thinly sliced
- 1 (28-ounce) can diced tomatoes, undrained
- 4 cups chicken broth
- 1/2 cup dry white wine
- Pinch of saffron threads

- 1 teaspoon dried thyme
- 1/2 teaspoon salt
- 1/4 teaspoon black pepper
- 1 pound assorted seafood (shrimp, mussels, clams, fish, etc.), cleaned and chopped
- 1/2 cup chopped fresh parsley

Method:

1. Build the Flavor Base: Heat olive oil in a large Dutch oven or pot over medium heat. Add the onion and cook until softened, about 5 minutes. Stir in the garlic and cook for 30 seconds, releasing the fragrant aroma. Add the fennel and cook for an additional 5 minutes, until softened and slightly golden.

2. Simmer in Goodness: Pour in the diced tomatoes, chicken broth, white wine, saffron threads, thyme, salt, and pepper. Bring to a simmer and cook for 15 minutes, allowing the flavors to meld.

3. Welcome the Sea: Add the chopped seafood and cook for 5-7 minutes, or until cooked through and opaque for fish and white for shellfish. Do not overcook to retain the tender texture.

4. Fresh Herb Finish: Stir in the chopped parsley and adjust seasonings if needed.

5. Serve with Sunshine: Ladle the steaming soup into bowls. Serve with crusty bread for dipping, grated Parmesan cheese, chopped basil, and rouille (if using) for an extra kick.

NUTRITIONAL INFORMATION (PER SERVING, APPROXIMATE) :

Calories: 350, Fat: 15g, Saturated Fat: 3g, Cholesterol: 120mg, Sodium: 400mg, Carbohydrates: 30g, Fiber: 2g, Sugar: 5g, Protein: 30g

CHAPTER TEN

PLANT-POWERED DELIGHTS

96. SPICED LENTIL SHEPHERD'S PIE WITH SMOKY TEMPEH CRUMBLES:.

97. ROASTED RATATOUILLE WITH CRISPY TOFU FETA:

98. LEMONY WHITE BEAN & ARTICHOKE SALAD WITH MINT:

99. STUFFED PORTOBELLO MUSHROOMS WITH QUINOA & SPINACH.

100.   CHICKPEA FRITTERS WITH TAHINI SAUCE & CUCUMBER SALAD

SPICED LENTIL SHEPHERD'S PIE WITH SMOKY TEMPEH CRUMBLES

Prep Time: 15 minutes **Cooking Time**: 50 minutes **Total Time**: 1 hour 5 minutes **Servings**: 4-6

Ingredients:

FOR THE LENTIL FILLING:

- 1 tablespoon olive oil
- 1 onion, chopped
- 2 cloves garlic, minced
- 1 cup green lentils, rinsed
- 1 celery stalk, chopped
- 1 carrot, chopped
- 1 teaspoon ground cumin
- 1/2 teaspoon dried thyme
- 1/4 teaspoon smoked paprika
- 1 (28-ounce) can diced tomatoes, undrained
- 4 cups vegetable broth
- 1/2 cup chopped fresh parsley

FOR THE SMOKY TEMPEH CRUMBLES:

- 1/2 block tempeh, crumbled
- 1 tablespoon olive oil
- 1/2 teaspoon smoked paprika
- 1/4 teaspoon onion powder
- 1/4 teaspoon garlic powder
- Salt and pepper to taste

FOR THE MASHED POTATOES:

- 4 large potatoes, peeled and cubed
- 1/2 cup milk (unsweetened almond milk works well)
- 2 tablespoons vegan butter
- Salt and pepper to taste

Method:

1. Let the Lentils Dance with Spices: Heat olive oil in a large Dutch oven or pot over medium heat. Add the onion and cook until softened, about 5 minutes. Stir in the garlic, cumin, thyme, and paprika, and cook for 30 seconds, releasing the fragrant aroma.

2. Welcome the Veggies and Grains: Add the lentils, celery, carrot, and diced tomatoes. Pour in the vegetable broth and bring to a simmer. Cover and cook for 20 minutes, or until the lentils are tender.

3. Smoky Tempeh Temptation: While the lentils simmer, prepare the tempeh crumbles. In a small bowl, combine crumbled tempeh, olive oil, smoked paprika, onion powder, garlic powder, salt, and pepper. Heat a skillet over medium heat and add the tempeh mixture. Cook for 5-7 minutes, stirring occasionally, until slightly crispy and golden brown.

4. Mash it Up for Creaminess: While the tempeh cooks, boil the cubed potatoes in a separate pot until tender. Drain and return to the pot with milk and vegan butter. Mash until smooth and creamy, seasoning with salt and pepper to taste.

5. Assemble the Flavor Symphony: Preheat oven to 400°F (200°C). Transfer the cooked lentils to a baking dish. Top with the smoky tempeh crumbles and spread the mashed potatoes evenly over the top.

6. Bake to Golden Perfection: Bake for 20-25 minutes, or until the mashed potatoes are lightly golden brown.

7. Serve with Sunshine: Let the shepherd's pie cool slightly before serving. Garnish with chopped parsley and dive into a heartwarming dish bursting with flavor and goodness.

NUTRITIONAL INFORMATION (PER SERVING, APPROXIMATE):

Calories: 400, Fat: 15g, Saturated Fat: 2g, Cholesterol: 0mg, Sodium: 450mg, Carbohydrates: 50g,, Fiber: 10g, Sugar: 5g, Protein: 25g

ROASTED RATATOUILLE WITH CRISPY TOFU FETA

Prep Time: 15 minutes **Cooking Time**: 45-50 minutes **Total Time**: 1 hour **Servings**: 4-6

Ingredients:

FOR THE ROASTED VEGETABLES:

- 1 eggplant, cubed
- 1 zucchini, cubed
- 1 red bell pepper, cubed
- 1 yellow bell pepper, cubed
- 1/4 cup olive oil
- 2 cloves garlic, minced
- 1/2 teaspoon dried oregano
- 1/2 teaspoon dried thyme
- Salt and pepper to taste

FOR THE CRISPY TOFU FETA:

- 1 block extra-firm tofu, drained and pressed
- 1/4 cup olive oil
- 1/4 cup nutritional yeast
- 1/4 cup crumbled feta cheese
- 1/4 teaspoon dried oregano
- 1/4 teaspoon garlic powder
- Salt and pepper to taste
- For Serving (optional):
- Chopped fresh parsley
- Fresh basil leaves
- Toasted pita bread

Method:

1. Prep the Veggie Stage: Preheat oven to 400°F (200°C). Toss the cubed eggplant, zucchini, bell peppers, olive oil, garlic, oregano, thyme, salt, and pepper in a large bowl until evenly coated. Spread the veggie mixture on a baking sheet in a single layer.

2. Roast to Radiant Beauty: Roast the vegetables for 40-45 minutes, or until tender and slightly caramelized, stirring occasionally.

3. Tofu Feta Transformation: While the veggies roast, crumble the pressed tofu into a small bowl. Drizzle with olive oil and massage it in to coat the tofu crumbles. In a separate bowl, combine nutritional yeast, crumbled feta cheese, oregano, garlic powder, salt, and pepper. Add this mixture to the coated tofu crumbles and toss to combine.

4. Spread Golden Goodness: Once the vegetables are roasted, sprinkle the tofu feta mixture evenly over them. Return the baking sheet to the oven and roast for an additional 5-7 minutes, or until the tofu crumbles are slightly golden brown and crispy.

5. Plate with Perfection: Transfer the vibrant roasted vegetables and crispy tofu feta to a serving dish. Garnish with chopped parsley and fresh basil leaves. Serve with toasted pita bread for scooping up the deliciousness.

NUTRITIONAL INFORMATION (PER SERVING, APPROXIMATE):

Calories: 350, Fat: 15g, Saturated Fat: 3g, Cholesterol: 5mg, Sodium: 400mg, Carbohydrates: 30g, Fiber: 5g, Sugar: 5g, Protein: 20g

Prep Time: 15 minutes **Cooking Time**: 0 (unless using canned beans) **Total Time**: 15 minutes **Servings**: 4-6

Ingredients:

FOR THE SALAD:

- 1 can (15 oz) cannellini beans, drained and rinsed (or 1 cup cooked cannellini beans)
- 1 (14 oz) can quartered artichoke hearts, drained and rinsed
- 1 cup cherry tomatoes, halved
- 1/2 cucumber, thinly sliced
- 1/4 cup chopped fresh parsley
- 2 tablespoons chopped fresh mint

FOR THE LEMON & OLIVE OIL DRESSING:

- 1/4 cup olive oil
- 2 tablespoons lemon juice
- 1/2 teaspoon Dijon mustard
- 1/4 teaspoon honey
- Salt and pepper to taste

Method:

- Gather the Sunshine: In a large bowl, combine the drained and rinsed cannellini beans, artichoke hearts, cherry tomatoes, cucumber, parsley, and mint.
- Whip Up the Lemony Magic: In a separate small bowl, whisk together the olive oil, lemon juice, Dijon mustard, and honey. Season with salt and pepper to taste.
- Dress with Flavor: Pour the lemon and olive oil dressing over the salad ingredients and toss gently to coat everything evenly.
- Let the Flavors Bloom: Let the salad stand for 5-10 minutes to allow the flavors to meld before serving.

NUTRITIONAL INFORMATION (PER SERVING, APPROXIMATE):

Calories: 250, Fat: 10g, Saturated Fat: 1g, Cholesterol: 0mg, Sodium: 400mg, Carbohydrates: 30g, Fiber: 5g, Sugar: 5g, Protein: 10g

STUFFED PORTOBELLO MUSHROOMS WITH QUINOA & SPINACH.

Prep Time: **15 minutes** Cooking Time: **25 minutes** Total Time: **40 minutes Servings: 4**

Ingredients:

FOR THE FILLING:

- 1 cup cooked quinoa
- 1 cup fresh spinach, chopped
- 1/2 cup sun-dried tomatoes, chopped
- 2 tablespoons pesto
- 1/4 cup crumbled feta cheese (optional)
- 1/4 cup grated Parmesan cheese
- 1/4 teaspoon dried oregano
- Salt and pepper to taste

FOR THE PORTOBELLOS:

- 4 large portobello mushrooms
- 1 tablespoon olive oil
- Salt and pepper to taste

Method:

1. Prep the Portobello Stage: Wipe the portobello mushrooms clean with a damp cloth. Remove the stems and gently scrape out the gills with a spoon. Drizzle each mushroom cap with olive oil and season generously with salt and pepper.
2. Build the Flavorful Filling: In a large bowl, combine the cooked quinoa, chopped spinach, sun-dried tomatoes, pesto, feta cheese (if using), Parmesan cheese, oregano, salt, and pepper. Mix well to combine.
3. Stuff with Goodness: Divide the quinoa mixture evenly among the portobello mushroom caps. Press down gently to ensure the filling is compact.

4. Roast to Perfection: Preheat oven to 400°F (200°C). Place the stuffed portobello mushrooms on a baking sheet and roast for 20-25 minutes, or until the quinoa is heated through and the mushrooms are tender.

5. Plate with Passion: Serve the stuffed portobello mushrooms warm, drizzled with any pan juices from the baking sheet. Garnish with fresh basil leaves or additional crumbled feta cheese (if using).

NUTRITIONAL INFORMATION (PER SERVING, APPROXIMATE):

Calories: 350, Fat: 15g, Saturated Fat: 3g, Cholesterol: 5mg, Sodium: 400mg, Carbohydrates: 30, Fiber: 5g, Sugar: 5g, Protein: 20g

Prep Time: 15 minutes **Cooking Time**: 20 minutes **Total Time**: 35 minutes **Servings**: 4-6

Ingredients:

FOR THE CHICKPEA FRITTERS:

- 1 (15 oz) can chickpeas, drained and rinsed
- 1/2 cup finely chopped onion
- 1/4 cup chopped fresh parsley
- 1/4 cup chickpea flour (or all-purpose flour)
- 1/2 teaspoon ground cumin
- 1/4 teaspoon paprika
- Salt and pepper to taste
- Canola oil for frying (about 1/2 inch depth)

FOR THE TAHINI SAUCE:

- 1/3 cup tahini
- 1/4 cup water
- 2 tablespoons lemon juice
- 1 clove garlic, minced
- 2 tablespoons olive oil
- Salt and pepper to taste

FOR THE CUCUMBER SALAD:

- 1 cucumber, thinly sliced
- 1/4 cup chopped red onion
- 2 tablespoons olive oil
- 1 tablespoon lemon juice
- 1/4 teaspoon dried oregano
- Salt and pepper to taste

Method:

1. Mash the Chickpea Goodness: In a food processor, pulse the chickpeas with the onion and parsley until a coarse mixture forms.

2. Spice it Up: Transfer the chickpea mixture to a bowl and stir in the chickpea flour, cumin, paprika, salt, and pepper.

3. Form the Fritter Fun: Heat the canola oil in a large skillet over medium heat. Wet your hands slightly and form the chickpea mixture into small patties, about 2 inches in diameter.

4. Fry to Golden Perfection: Carefully place the fritters in the hot oil and cook for 3-4 minutes per side, or until golden brown and crispy. Drain on paper towels.

5. Whip Up the Tahini Dream: In a bowl, whisk together the tahini, water, lemon juice, garlic, olive oil, salt, and pepper until smooth and creamy.

6. Cucumber Salad Refreshment: Toss the sliced cucumber, red onion, olive oil, lemon juice, oregano, salt, and pepper in a small bowl.

7. Plate with Passion: Arrange the crispy chickpea fritters on a platter. Drizzle with the creamy tahini sauce and top with a spoonful of the refreshing cucumber salad.

NUTRITIONAL INFORMATION (PER SERVING, APPROXIMATE) :

Calories: 250, Fat: 10g, Saturated Fat: 1g, Cholesterol: 0mg, Sodium: 400mg, Carbohydrates: 30g, Fiber: 5g, Sugar: 5g, Protein: 10g

CHAPTER ELEVEN

DESSERT

101. **GREEK YOGURT PANNA COTTA WITH HONEY & PISTACHIOS:**

102. **TURKISH HONEY BAKLAVA WITH WALNUTS AND CINNAMON**

103. **ALMOND & ORANGE BLOSSOM SEMIFREDDO**

104. **RICOTTA CANNOLI WITH LEMON RICOTTA & CANDIED CITRUS:**

105. **SPICED FIG & WALNUT TART WITH YOGURT CRUST**

GREEK YOGURT PANNA COTTA WITH HONEY & PISTACHIOS

Prep Time: 10 minutes **Chill Time**: 4 hours (minimum) **Total Time**: 4 hours 10 minutes **Servings**: 4-6

Ingredients:

FOR THE PANNA COTTA:

- 16 oz plain Greek yogurt (whole milk or low-fat)
- 1/2 cup heavy cream
- 1/4 cup granulated sugar
- 1 teaspoon vanilla extract
- 6 sheets gelatin, softened in cold water for 5 minutes

FOR THE HONEY & PISTACHIO TOPPING:

- 1/4 cup honey
- 1/4 cup chopped pistachios

Method:

1. Bloom the Gelatin: In a small bowl, sprinkle the gelatin sheets over 1/4 cup cold water and let them soften for 5 minutes.
2. Warm the Cream: In a medium saucepan, heat the heavy cream and sugar over medium heat until the sugar dissolves. Be careful not to boil.
3. Infuse the Yogurt: Remove the pan from heat and stir in the softened gelatin until completely dissolved. Then, whisk in the Greek yogurt and vanilla extract until smooth and combined.
4. Pour and Chill: Divide the panna cotta mixture evenly among individual serving glasses or ramekins. Cover with plastic wrap and refrigerate for at least 4 hours, or until set.
5. Honey & Pistachio Bliss: Just before serving, drizzle each panna cotta with a spoonful of honey and sprinkle with chopped pistachios.

NUTRITIONAL INFORMATION (PER SERVING, APPROXIMATE) :

Calories: 250, Fat: 15g, Saturated Fat: 5g, Cholesterol: 25mg, Sodium: 150mg, Carbohydrates: 25g, Fiber: 0g, Sugar: 20g, Protein: 8g

TURKISH HONEY BAKLAVA WITH WALNUTS AND CINNAMON

Prep Time: 20 minutes **Cookngi Time**: 1 hour 20 minutes **Total Time**: 1 hour 40 minutes **Servings:** 8-10

Ingredients:

FOR THE BAKLAVA:

- 1 (1 pound) package phyllo dough, thawed and at room temperature
- 1/2 cup melted butter
- 1 cup walnuts, finely chopped
- 1/2 cup sugar
- 1 tablespoon ground cinnamon
- 1/4 teaspoon ground cloves (optional)

FOR THE HONEY SYRUP:

- 1 cup water
- 1 cup honey
- 1 lemon peel, zest only

Method:

1.
   Prep the Walnut Symphony: Preheat oven to 350°F (175°C). Combine chopped walnuts, sugar, cinnamon, and cloves (if using) in a bowl.
2. Assemble the Phyllo Layers: Brush a 9x13 inch baking dish with melted butter. Carefully unfold the phyllo dough and lay one sheet flat in the pan, brushing it with butter. Repeat with 8-10 sheets, creating overlapping layers.
3. Sprinkle the Filling Bliss: Spread half of the walnut mixture evenly over the layered phyllo. Dot with melted butter. Layer another 8-10 sheets of phyllo on top, brushing each with butter. Sprinkle the remaining walnut mixture on top.

4. Finish the Phyllo Canvas: Top with the final 8-10 sheets of phyllo, again brushing each with butter. Carefully fold any overhanging edges into the pan. Using a sharp knife, score the baklava into diamond-shaped pieces, cutting through all the layers but not into the bottom of the pan. Drizzle the top generously with melted butter.

5. Bake to Golden Perfection: Bake the baklava for 1 hour, or until golden brown and slightly crisp.

6. Prepare the Honeyed Embrace: While the baklava bakes, combine water, honey, and lemon zest in a saucepan. Bring to a simmer and cook for 5 minutes, until slightly thickened. Remove from heat and let cool slightly.

7. Infuse with Sweetness: As soon as the baklava comes out of the oven, slowly and evenly pour the warm honey syrup over the hot baklava. Allow the syrup to soak in for at least 30 minutes before serving.

8. Serve with Sunshine: Let the baklava cool slightly before cutting and serving the diamond-shaped pieces. Enjoy warm or at room temperature, adorned with chopped walnuts and a sprinkle of cinnamon, if desired.

NUTRITIONAL INFORMATION (PER SERVING, APPROXIMATE):

Calories: 350, Fat: 15g, Saturated Fat: 3g, Cholesterol: 5mg, Sodium: 150mg, Carbohydrates: 40g, Fiber: 2g, Sugar: 25g, Protein: 5g

ALMOND & ORANGE BLOSSOM SEMIFREDDO

Prep Time: 15 minutes **Chill Time**: 4 hours (minimum) **Total Time**: 4 hours 15 minutes **Servings**: 6-8

Ingredients:

FOR THE SEMIFREDDO:

- 1 cup heavy cream
- 1/4 cup granulated sugar
- 1/4 teaspoon almond extract
- 1 tablespoon orange blossom water
- 4 large egg yolks

- 1/2 cup chopped toasted almonds
- For the Whipped Cream (optional):
- 1 cup heavy cream
- 2 tablespoons powdered sugar
- 1/2 teaspoon vanilla extract

FOR GARNISH (OPTIONAL):

- Chopped toasted almonds
- Candied orange peel

- Fresh mint leaves

Method:

1. Whip the Cream to Cloud Nine: In a large bowl, whisk together the heavy cream and sugar until stiff peaks form. Set aside.

2. Infuse the Almond & Orange Delight: In a separate bowl, whisk together the almond extract and orange blossom water. In another bowl, whisk the egg yolks until pale and fluffy. Gradually add the sugar to the egg yolks and whisk until thick and lemon-colored. Gently fold in the almond and orange blossom mixture.

3. Creamy Fusion: Using a spatula, gently fold the whipped cream into the egg yolk mixture until just combined. Be careful not to overmix. Gently fold in the chopped toasted almonds.

193

4. Chill to Perfection: Transfer the semifreddo mixture to a loaf pan or individual serving molds. Cover with plastic wrap and refrigerate for at least 4 hours, or until frozen solid.

5. Whip Up the Optional Delight: Just before serving, whip the heavy cream with powdered sugar and vanilla extract until stiff peaks form.

6. Plate with Sunshine: Slice the chilled semifreddo and arrange on serving plates. Top with a dollop of whipped cream (if using) and garnish with chopped toasted almonds, candied orange peel, and fresh mint leaves, if desired.

NUTRITIONAL INFORMATION (PER SERVING, APPROXIMATE):

Calories: 300, Fat: 20g, Saturated Fat: 10g, Cholesterol: 120mg, Sodium: 50mg, Carbohydrates: 25g

Fiber: 1g, Sugar: 20g, Protein: 5g

RICOTTA CANNOLI WITH LEMON RICOTTA & CANDIED CITRUS

Prep Time: 20 minutes **Cooking Time**: 15 minutes **Total Time**: 35 minutes **Servings**: 8-10

Ingredients:

FOR THE CANNOLI SHELLS:

- 1 cup all-purpose flour
- 1/4 cup unsweetened cocoa powder
- 1/4 teaspoon salt
- 1/3 cup ricotta cheese
- 1 large egg yolk
- 1/4 teaspoon vanilla extract
- Canola oil for frying

FOR THE LEMON RICOTTA FILLING:

- 1 cup whole-milk ricotta cheese, chilled for at least 2 hours
- 1/4 cup powdered sugar
- 1 tablespoon lemon juice
- 1/4 teaspoon grated lemon zest
- 1/4 cup chopped candied orange or lemon peel

FOR FINISHING:

- Powdered sugar for dusting
- Additional candied citrus peel for garnish (optional)

Method:

1. Mix the Doughy Magic: In a medium bowl, whisk together the flour, cocoa powder, and salt. In a separate bowl, whisk together the ricotta cheese, egg yolk, and vanilla extract until smooth. Add the wet ingredients to the dry ingredients and mix until a soft dough forms. Knead the dough briefly on a lightly floured surface until smooth and elastic.

2. Chill Out, Dough: Wrap the dough in plastic wrap and refrigerate for at least 30 minutes, or up to overnight.

3. Shape the Cannoli Canvases: Roll out the chilled dough on a lightly floured surface to about 1/16-inch thickness. Cut into 3-inch rounds. Wrap each round around a cannoli form, sealing the seam with a dab of water.

4. Fry to Golden Perfection: Heat the canola oil in a deep fryer or large pot to 360°F (180°C). Carefully fry the cannoli shells for 1-2 minutes each, or until golden brown. Drain on paper towels and let cool completely before removing the forms.

5. Lemon Ricotta Bliss: In a bowl, whisk together the chilled ricotta cheese, powdered sugar, lemon juice, and lemon zest until smooth and creamy. Gently fold in the chopped candied citrus peel.

6. Fill with Sunshine: Pipe or spoon the lemon ricotta filling into the cooled cannoli shells. Dust with powdered sugar and garnish with additional candied citrus peel, if desired.

NUTRITIONAL INFORMATION (PER SERVING, APPROXIMATE):

Calories: 250, Fat: 10g, Saturated Fat: 3g, Cholesterol: 25mg, Sodium: 150mg, Carbohydrates: 30g, Fiber: 1g, Sugar: 20g, Protein: 5g

SPICED FIG & WALNUT TART WITH YOGURT CRUST

Prep Time: 20 minutes **Cooking Time**: 50 minutes **Total Time**: 70 minutes   **Servings:** 8-10

Ingredients:

FOR THE YOGURT CRUST:

- 1 1/2 cups all-purpose flour
- 1/2 cup plain Greek yogurt
- 1/4 cup cold unsalted butter, cubed
- 1/4 teaspoon salt

FOR THE SPICED FIG & WALNUT FILLING:

- 12 fresh figs, sliced
- 1/4 cup chopped walnuts
- 1/4 cup honey
- 1 tablespoon lemon juice
- 1/2 teaspoon ground cinnamon
- 1/4 teaspoon ground clove

Method:

1. Chill Out, Dough: In a large bowl, whisk together the flour and salt. Using a pastry cutter or your fingers, work in the cold butter until crumbly. Stir in the Greek yogurt until a dough forms. Wrap the dough in plastic wrap and refrigerate for at least 30 minutes.
2. Preheat the Oven: Preheat oven to 375°F (190°C).
3. Roll Out the Creamy Canvas: On a lightly floured surface, roll out the chilled dough to a 12-inch circle. Carefully transfer the dough to a 9-inch tart pan, pressing it evenly into the bottom and sides. Trim off any excess dough.
4. Prep the Figgy Goodness: In a bowl, combine the sliced figs, chopped walnuts, honey, lemon juice, cinnamon, and clove. Toss to coat the figs evenly.

5. Fill with Sunshine: Spread the fig mixture over the bottom of the chilled crust.

6. Bake to Golden Perfection: Bake the tart for 40-50 minutes, or until the crust is golden brown and the filling is bubbly. Let cool slightly before cutting and serving.

7. Plate with Passion: Slice the tart into wedges and arrange on serving plates. Garnish with whipped cream, vanilla ice cream, or a drizzle of honey, if desired.

NUTRITIONAL INFORMATION (PER SERVING, APPROXIMATE) :

Calories: 300, Fat: 15g, Saturated Fat: 5g, Cholesterol: 25mg, Sodium: 150mg, Carbohydrates: 35g

Fiber: 3g, Sugar: 25g, Protein: 5g

CHAPTER TWELVE

30 - DAY MEAL PLAN

Week 1: GREEK ISLAND ESCAPE

Breakfast (Greek Sunrises) :

Monday: Creamy Greek Yogurt with Honey, Granola, and Berries

Tuesday: Scrambled Eggs with Spinach and Feta, Toasted Pita Bread

Wednesday: Whole-Wheat Pancakes with Fresh Figs and Ricotta Cheese

Thursday: Oatmeal with Chopped Nuts and Seeds, Drizzled with Olive Oil

Friday: Smoothie with Greek Yogurt, Banana, Spinach, and Almond Milk

Lunch (Aegean Breezes):

Monday: Chickpea Salad Sandwich on Pita Bread with Cucumber, Tomato, and Tzatziki

Tuesday: Quinoa Salad with Roasted Vegetables and Grilled Chicken

Wednesday: Leftover Greek Lasagna with Spinach and Ricotta Cheese

Thursday: Lentil Soup with Whole-Wheat Bread

Friday: Tuna Salad with Greek Twist: Olives, Celery, Dill, and Lemon Juice

Dinner (Golden Aegean Delights):

Monday: Baked Salmon with Lemon & Herbs, Roasted Potatoes, and Green Beans

Tuesday: Greek Chicken Kabobs with Grilled Vegetables and Couscous

Wednesday: Shrimp Scampi with Whole-Wheat Pasta and Light Tomato Sauce

Thursday: Vegetarian Moussaka with Lentils and Portobello Mushrooms

Friday: Grilled Vegetable Pizza with Feta Cheese and Olives

WEEK 2: ITALIAN INTERLUDE

BREAKFAST (TUSCAN MORNINGS):

Monday: Italian Frittata with Sausage, Peppers, and Onions

Tuesday: Ricotta Pancakes with Fruit Compote and Maple Syrup

Wednesday: Overnight Oats with Chia Seeds, Yogurt, and Berries

Thursday: Eggs Florentine on Whole-Wheat English Muffins

Friday: Smoothie with Peanut Butter, Banana, Spinach, and Milk

LUNCH (ROMAN RENDEZVOUS):

Monday: Panini with Mozzarella, Pesto, and Sun-Dried Tomatoes

Tuesday: Antipasto Salad with Grilled Chicken, Artichchoke Hearts, and Olives

Wednesday: Minestrone Sozup with Crusty Bread

Thursday: Tuna Salad with Chopped Apples, Celery, and Walnuts

Friday: Leftover Pasta from Dinner

DINNER (A FEAST UNDER THE TUSCAN SUN):

Monday: Lemon Ricotta Ravioli with Roasted Vegetables and Pine Nuts

Tuesday: Baked Chicken Parmesan with Roasted Asparagus and Quinoa

Wednesday: Spicy Sausage and White Bean Soup with Crusty Bread

Thursday: Salmon with Pesto, Grilled Zucchini, and Brown Rice

Friday: Vegetarian Pizza with Roasted Eggplant, Fresh Tomatoes, and Mozzarella Cheese

WEEK 3: SPANISH FIESTA

BREAKFAST (FLAMENCO FLAVORS):

Monday: Tortilla Española (Spanish Potato Omelet) with Salad

Tuesday: Whole-Wheat Toast with Avocado and Smoked Salmon

Wednesday: Smoothie with Mango, Pineapple, Greek Yogurt, and Coconut Milk

Thursday: Scrambled Eggs with Chorizo and Bell Peppers

Friday: Oatmeal with Chopped Dates and Almonds

LUNCH (PICNIC IN THE PLAZA):

Monday: Gazpacho with Grilled Shrimp and Crusty Bread

Tuesday: Chicken and Chorizo Paella with Peppers and Peas

Wednesday: Black Bean and Corn Salad with Whole-Wheat Tortillas

Thursday: Tuna Salad with Chopped Peppers, Onions, and Olives

Friday: Leftover Paella

DINNER (MEDITERRANEAN MAGIC BY THE SEA):

Monday: Grilled Fish with Roasted Vegetables and Aioli Sauce

Tuesday: Paella Valenciana with Chicken, Seafood, and Saffron

Wednesday: Chicken Skewers with Roasted Peppers and Onions, Served with Grilled Pita Bread

Thursday: Vegetarian Tortilla Española with Mushrooms and Spinach

Friday: Shrimp Cocktail with Avocado and a Tangy Citrus Sauce

WEEK 4: MEDITERRANEAN MEDLEY

BREAKFAST (MORNING MOSAIC):

Monday: Yogurt Parfait with Granola, Fruit, and Honey

Tuesday: Whole-Wheat Waffles with Berries and Ricotta Cheese

Wednesday: Scrambled Eggs with Feta Cheese and

GLOSSARY

- **Olive Oil:** An essential ingredient in Greek cuisine, olive oil may be found in a variety of dishes, including salads, dips, and stir-fries. The best olive oil is extra virgin olive oil, which is valued for both its health advantages and delicious taste.

- **Feta Cheese**: This crumbly, sour sheep's milk cheese gives a creamy, salty touch to a lot of recipes. Crumbled feta fills savory pastries, garnishes salads, and tops moussaka.

- Plump and purple, kalamata olives have a deep, salty taste. They enhance salads, fill dolmas, and give stews and braises more flavor.

- **Tzatziki**: This well-known dip made with yogurt, garlic, cucumber, dill, and olive oil makes a cool, creamy side dish to go with grilled meats, veggies, and pita bread.

- **Grilling:** An essential component of Greek cooking, grilling gives meats, fish, and vegetables a deliciously soft, smokey char. A few examples include grilled halloumi cheese, grilled octopus, and souvlaki skewers.

- **Roasting**: Roasting enhances the aromas of meat and poultry and brings out the inherent sweetness of vegetables. Greek cuisine often consists of roasted potatoes, lamb, eggplant, and tomatoes.

- **Braising**: This slow-cooking method creates foods that are so tender that they melt in your tongue by using liquid and mild heat to break down stiff fibers. A famous example is beef stifado, which is slow-cooked with tomatoes, onions, and red wine.

- **Olive Oil**: Olive oil has taste all by itself and is used for more than simply cooking. Greeks liberally sprinkle it over veggies, salads, and even plain bread to bring out the flavors of the other foods. The finished meal might be significantly impacted by the kind of olive oil used. Strong extra virgin olive oil gives a hint of spice, while softer oils complement delicate tastes beautifully.

- **Feta Cheese**: Greek cooking showcases feta's adaptability. Its creamy texture lends richness to savory pies and pasta dishes, while its salty undertones counterbalance the sweetness of tomatoes in salads. Younger feta is tangier and milder, whereas aged feta has a stronger taste.

- **Kalamata Olives**: A variety of meals get richness from the salty punch of Kalamata olives. They may be filled with herbs and spices for a tasty delicacy, or eaten whole as part of an appetizer spread. They can also be diced and added to salads.

- **Tzatziki**: This adaptable dip is more than just a complement. It may be mixed into soups to provide a hint of creaminess and acidity, diluted and used as a salad dressing, or spooned over grilled meats and veggies.

- **Grilling**: Direct heat and simplicity are the hallmarks of Greek grilling methods. Meats skewered with minimum seasonings so that the tastes of the meat itself may be highlighted. The smoky sear on the vegetables balances their sweetness.

- **Roasting**: To caramelize vegetables and infuse them with olive oil and herbs, Greek roasting often calls for high heat and extended cooking durations. Whole vegetables, such as potatoes and cauliflower, become delicious and tender, while meats and poultry receive crispy skin and juicy insides.

- **Braising**: Braising turns harder portions of meat into succulent, mouthwatering dishes. The braising liquid gains depth and complexity with the addition of herbs, spices, and vegetables, which results in a rich and savory sauce that enhances the whole meal.

CONCLUSION

To sum up, the "Mediterranean Refresh Cookbook" is a wonderful exploration of one of the most cherished culinary traditions on earth. With careful attention to taste, whole foods, and a dedication to health, this cookbook offers you more than just a list of delectable recipes— it also acts as a manual for adopting a more balanced and healthful way of living.

Focusing on the well-known Mediterranean diet, the cookbook promotes a balanced eating style that highlights the availability of fresh produce, lean meats, and heart-healthy fats. The well chosen dishes showcase the gastronomic tapestry woven by the sun-kissed lands and turquoise seas of the Mediterranean, reflecting the great variety of the cuisine.

In addition to its delicious recipes, the "Mediterranean Refresh Cookbook" is a great resource for anybody looking to improve their eating habits. The book deftly combines cultural insights, dietary data, and useful advice to enable readers to make health-conscious decisions while enjoying the delights of the Mediterranean diet.

Essentially, this cookbook is a travel companion for health and culinary pleasure rather than just a compilation of recipes. The "Mediterranean Refresh Cookbook" allows you to rediscover the pleasure of cooking and eating in a manner that feeds both body and spirit, regardless of your level of culinary experience. So take off on this tasty journey and let the alluring flavors and scents of the Mediterranean to revive your sense of taste and wellbeing.

Made in United States
Troutdale, OR
04/06/2024

19001325R00117